# OH CHURCH, WHY SO MUCH LIKE A CIRCUS?

ROSS MORGAN

# Table of Contents

Copyright . . . . . . . . . . . . . . . . . . . . . . . . . . . . . . . . . . . . . . *I*

Introduction . . . . . . . . . . . . . . . . . . . . . . . . . . . . . . . . . . . .*II*

Acknowledgments. . . . . . . . . . . . . . . . . . . . . . . . . . . . . . . *IV*

Scripture Used. . . . . . . . . . . . . . . . . . . . . . . . . . . . . . . . . *VI*

Finding the Right Way. . . . . . . . . . . . . . . . . . . . . . . . . . . . *1*

Coming Into His Grace . . . . . . . . . . . . . . . . . . . . . . . . . . *10*

Growing Up in Him . . . . . . . . . . . . . . . . . . . . . . . . . . . . *13*

Allowing God to Do It the Right Way . . . . . . . . . . . . . . . *16*

Presumption in the Church. . . . . . . . . . . . . . . . . . . . . . . *21*

Who is Building the Church? . . . . . . . . . . . . . . . . . . . . . *29*

Bring Back God's Glory The Right Way. . . . . . . . . . . . . . *36*

Spending Time with God and His Word . . . . . . . . . . . . . *40*

When God says No, we need to hear it. . . . . . . . . . . . . . . *45*

Huff and Puff of Man's Endeavours. . . . . . . . . . . . . . . . . *54*

Give us a King like other nations . . . . . . . . . . . . . . . . . . *60*

School of hard knocks. . . . . . . . . . . . . . . . . . . . . . . . . . . *74*

Which God? . . . . . . . . . . . . . . . . . . . . . . . . . . . . . . . . . *83*

*God's Commandments* . . . . . . . . . . . . . . . . . . . . . . . . . . . . . *91*

*Savaging the Flock* . . . . . . . . . . . . . . . . . . . . . . . . . . . . . *101*

*Learning To Tell the Difference* . . . . . . . . . . . . . . . . . . . . *110*

*Be Careful What Spirit Controls You* . . . . . . . . . . . . . . . . . *127*

*Be On Guard and Let Jesus Rule* . . . . . . . . . . . . . . . . . . . . *138*

*Responsibility of Leaders* . . . . . . . . . . . . . . . . . . . . . . . . . *145*

*Let's Get Away From the Pig Pens* . . . . . . . . . . . . . . . . . . *151*

*Let's Get Back To Rightly Dividing the Word* . . . . . . . . . . . . *154*

*Good Seed and Bad Seed* . . . . . . . . . . . . . . . . . . . . . . . . . *171*

*Bringing Again the Acceptable Sacrifice* . . . . . . . . . . . . . . . *173*

# Copyright

Copyright © 2016 Ross Morgan

This work is copyright. Apart from any use permitted under the Copyright Act 1968, no part may be reproduced by any process, nor may any other exclusive right be exercised, without the permission of Ross John Morgan of 5 Nannatee Way, Wanneroo, WA 6065, email: rmo28458@bigpond.net.au

ISBN 978-0-646-95480-6

Printed and bound in Australia by Lightning Source Australia

Designed by POP Creative

POP Creative is a design and marketing agency run by Colosoul Group Inc, a not for profit art and media organisation primarily based in Perth, Western Australia. The agency connects corporate clients with the expertise of innovative and talented creative artists.

popcreative@colosoul.com.au

popcreativedesign.com

# Introduction

Being a Christian for some time now, I believe the Lord has shown me so much of the way He builds His church. It started off right back at the beginning of my work with Him! Being a new born babe I didn't really comprehend what was going on at times, which is quite understandable, as new born babes don't. As time went by and my desire to walk with Him got stronger, I guess, you get a little bit more mature and start to grow in Him. Now, with this comes pain, growing pain, which is not that nice at times, but a necessity that we all have to endure so it can teach us that our flesh doesn't achieve much in the eyes of our Lord, in fact He wants to kill it off. I'm sure that many will find this book very controversial, but it's only controversial to those that don't agree with what I have written. Now, what I have written, not to the letter, but to the spirit, I believe is truth. Now, that's a big statement some would say and they are right, truth and grace came with Jesus according to the bible, and combined together will set us free, but only if we put them into practice. Jesus is building His church and we must hear what the Holy Spirit is saying to that church and come to an understanding of the way He wants it built. There is no qualms about it, as the saying goes, "Unless the Lord builds the house we might as well stop right now, because in many cases, we are not doing it right and our endeavours will come to nothing", well that's my version anyway. As it was with Mary, Jesus' mother, when she didn't always understand what he meant, when at times he said or did things, she hid them in her heart. This is something we all have to do and over time it should gel together to bring meaning of what God is saying to us. But, and I mean But we need time out to hear what He is saying. Being part of the body of Christ, we all have our part to play. Writing this book is one small part on my account, if possible, to help the church of Jesus Christ to come to a place of seeing that not all things are kosher, and not all things are right in His Church. Not all that seems to be of Him are, indeed, not of Him at all! As you read through the pages I hope that the spirit in which I write them will come through helping others come to a place of greater freedom and liberty in Jesus our Lord.

# Acknowledgments

Writing a book is not that easy, well to me its not, as I am not that good on a computer, although I believe I have got better, I think. It started off by putting pen to paper, which is ok but the trouble with that is I am the only one that can read it! A friend of mine, Tricia Ray said she would help out by printing some of it on the computer, which was fantastic, but its quite time consuming and Tricia herself has an extremely busy schedule in her own business. The lady who works for me, Louise Richards said she would take over as I had nowhere near finished the book. Again did a fantastic job. An old friend of mine had just come back from Canada and told another lady about my book, well she rang me and asked if she could help. This blew me away and being an English teacher and a person that loves the Lord I said yes. Elsje Maassen, again a person with a busy schedule put a lot of time and effort into the book. It never ceases to amaze me how the Lord works, a very good friend of mine, someone I grew up with in the Lord but hadn't seen for many years, out of the blue, rang me to have lunch with him. Over lunch he said his wife whom I also knew, said that she had edited a few books and said would I like her to edit mine. Of course I would. Paul and Kaye Host as I said go way back and I knew they were strong, stable Christians.

All these folk have been a real inspiration and help to me, the time and effort put in by them is priceless (if you find any spelling mistakes in the book, blame them). David Moore and his daughter, Reneisse, I would really like to acknowledge in a big way. These folk have been great prayer partners with me over some time now and have helped by their prayers and encouragement. There is another person that has been a great encouragement to me, whom I would like to thank from the bottom of my heart, is a Kiwi lady by the name of Annie Lovelock. I knew Annie way, way back growing up in New Zealand, her brothers and I were great mates, and still am. Annie and one of the brothers became Christians some years ago and as we got reacquainted, started to send Annie some of my unfinished works. She told me that she got a lot out of them and really encouraged me to finish the book and get it in print. The bible says that Jesus left the best to last and I am doing the same. Losing their mother to cancer in July 2008 really had a big impact on my two kids, Tanya and Stephen, as well as myself. Family is so, so important and it's made me realise this, to a greater degree, because of what we went through. I would like to acknowledge my children, even though at times it seems Satan himself was trying to pull us apart, but with God's help, we as a family have grown stronger and stronger. Going through this type of thing has made me see a little clearer, that in Christ Jesus all things are possible and I would like to acknowledge Him above all else!

# Scripture Used

NEW INTERNATIONAL VERION - study bible (NIV)

NEW REVISED STANDARD VERSION (NRSV)

REVISED STANDARD VERSION (RSV)

KING JAMES VERSION (KJV)

THE LIVING BIBLE (TLB)

*All quotes referenced

# 1

# Finding the Right Way

I was bought up a Catholic and attended parish schools and church, I began to hate this religion with a passion. I found it was boring and lifeless. At primary school I remember having a class that I had to attend for a week at the local Catholic Church. We sat in long hard pews and sang the hymns while repeating the Hail Mary over and over; it was horrible, followed by more hymns and other themes that I can't really remember now.

The education part of the school was okay: however I wasn't a very bright student. My mind was always wandering off thinking about fishing with my Dad and brothers, or if I wasn't thinking about fishing I was thinking about hunting. I loved the outdoors and school always felt like an inconvenience; it seemed to get in the way of what I really liked doing. I grew up in New Zealand (NZ) and I was surrounded by hills and mountains with plenty of game abounding in them. The seas and rivers were filled with plenty of fish too. New Zealand was and still is a camping, hiking, fishing and hunting paradise, a beautiful country.

Mum and Dad went to the local Catholic Church, as Mum was raised a Catholic but Dad became one later on in life, leaving the

Church of England. My brothers, sister and I went to the church with my parents from a young age. I felt like we were brainwashed to believe that the Catholic Church was the truth - the right way to reach God. If we missed church on Sunday, it was classed as a mortal sin; we were not allowed meat on Fridays and other consequences seemed to govern the way we should live. Most of my friends were bought up Catholic and so they were the ones I hung around with. I remember coming back and forth from school, passing kids from the other schools. We used to yell out to them, "Protestant dogs stink like frogs" and they would yell back at us "Catholic dogs stink like frogs" and sometimes a fight would break out. My friend Rod Sutcliff, whom I've known for about thirty-five years told me he used to yell out similar things at Catholic kids. He also told me that his mates and he also threw stones, as well as the abuse. Rod, being from Perth one couldn't expect anything else, could one?

    Behind our house was a small farm that belonged to the church; out on the property was a convent where some young girls lived with nuns who took care of them. I'm not sure if the girls were orphaned or just wayward kids. Out the front of the convent was quite a large area for parking and a driveway, where kids from school had to go over some evenings in Lent to participate in the "Stations of the Cross". The priests were in their robes and the nuns wore their black habits; this would have been the mid 1950's. When it began to get dark, the priests would carry a cross on a long brass pole while the rest of us followed behind them carrying candles. We all walked two by two singing and chanting spooky sounding hymns. I hated doing this so much I just couldn't wait to go home.

After finishing primary school I was then sent to a Catholic high school. It was an agricultural college with a lot of buildings around the grounds. It also had a working farm where many of the farm boys could brush up their agricultural skills, and learn new ones. The college catered for boarders as well as day boys but it didn't seem to do me much good as I wasn't that interested in being there. The college was a few kilometres from my home and I went there with some kids who lived down the road from me. We would either travel by train or by bike. It was a very old English style college and the class rooms were very spacious with high ceilings. The rooms had large windows and when you looked out of them you could see playing fields for rugby and cricket. It was a very beautiful layout of buildings and playing fields, which sloped down to a line of poplar trees that formed a boundary. From there the farm started and continued west to the Hutt River. The kids who were sent to the college to board mostly came from farms all over New Zealand. The day boys used to call the boarders scabs or scabby boys as a lot of them had pimples or scabby things on their faces, most likely from overeating the chocolate they used to smuggle into their dorms and eat late at night.

The college was an all boys' school and one thing that I envied most was that the non-catholic boys didn't have to go to church or do the Catholicism instruction which catholic kids had to. I can't remember if we did religious studies everyday but it seemed to be quite a lot of the time. We were instructed about the Holy Catholic Church, the Mother of Jesus and the Pope. We were also instructed about the many saints and somewhere in there Jesus Christ got a mention. I do remember a light hearted moment when one of the boys asked the priest, who was teaching what abortion was. One of the other boys piped and up said, "A rough ride on a motorbike?" To be honest with you, despite what we read and hear now about some priests being involved with sexual abuse of children, I cannot remember anything like that happening during my school years. I found that most of the priests were good blokes but I just hated the religion. Somewhere along the line, something of God and Jesus must have filtered through to me and for that I am eternally grateful.

Leaving high school at 15, I got into the carpentry trade, promising myself I'd never return to the Catholic Church again. Even though the saying was if they get you at a young age then they've got you for life, well, they weren't getting this bloke! As I have said before, I loved the outdoors, fishing and hunting. I met two brothers Geoff and Murray Wilkinson who hunted with dogs to catch wild pigs. Up until this time I had only hunted with a rifle. To understand why in New Zealand, hunting and fishing is such a popular way of life for many people, game animals such as many types of deer, pigs, goats, rabbits, possums, etc were bought into the bush by the first white settlers to provide food as well as sport for the upper class people (so called) who mainly came from mother England. This unfortunately created, later on, a massive problem for the environment!

On the high country and mountain ranges of the south island, Chamois, which is a type of antelope from Austria; and Thar, a type of a big goat from India and Nepal, were also liberated. Wallabies from Australia were also set free in parts of both Islands, and the problem occurred because the New Zealand terrain is so steep and the bush is so dense; the animals over-bred quickly, getting out of control and then became pests. Growing up there, we were encouraged by the government to kill as many wild animals as possible; otherwise the land environment was going to severely suffer. We didn't need a licence to hunt the animals but we did for the rifles or shoot guns we owned. In those days it was very easy to get a firearm licence, I'm not so sure what it's like today? New Zealand has no natural animals, they were all introduced but it does have many types of birds and creepy crawlies. Thankfully there are no snakes to keep an eye out for, we let Australia have them.

Hunting, fishing, hiking and camping were a way of life for many of us and I really got into it in my teens. Something inside of me was really looking for what life was all about; the church left a great void in me that needed filling. As a young lad, sometimes some friends and I would go down to a beach place called Paraparaumu (get your tongue around that one). Mum and Dad had a beach cottage there right near the coast as Dad was mad on fishing! We mostly went there on some weekends as well as Christmas and Easter holidays. I remember some of the other churchies who were nearby would come to the beach and have gospel outreaches. Mostly they would show some gospel films and give a message afterwards. My friends and I used to go along, not so much for the films, but to check out the birds (girls) that went along as well.

My friends Geoff and Murray Wilkinson were not bought up in the same church as me, but that didn't matter, they loved the outdoors and that's all that mattered. I remember being out with them one time and we were in the bush sitting in an opening on the side of a hill. The sun was coming up and we were warming ourselves after coming off a cold morning. We were talking and waiting for the dogs to come back or start barking to let us know they had found a wild pig. After a while one of the blokes commented, "Gee, God makes things fantastic!" When he said this we all looked at the hills and surrounding bush. My ears pricked up as I didn't know that he believed in God or even think, maybe there could be a God! This made me stop and contemplate that maybe there was something to believe in?

Some time later a group of us were hunting in another bushland area, we were chatting and mucking round and in conversation one of the blokes said "Jesus Christ" in a swearing type of a way. It felt like a dagger going into my heart but I couldn't understand why it affected me. I was definitely searching for something but I was not sure for what. After I finished my carpentry apprenticeship I decided to go full time into wild pig hunting since it was more my passion. I would be hunting to sell the meat as I saw the opportunity in it, people from Europe wanted to buy the wild game from New Zealand and it wasn't only wild boar they were after but deer, Chamois, Thar and anything else they could get their hands on. Since it was something that I really enjoyed doing, being in the out doors and something that was going to bring in some cash, then it was a perfect job for me.

I went and lived in a town named Wanganui on the west coast about a quarter of the way up the North Island not far from a small town called Raetihi, which is situated inland. From Raetihi, the bloke I was hunting with used to go into a place called the Mangapoura Valley, from the upper end of it. We would travel by car from Wanganui to Raetihi over sealed roads and from there over gravel bush roads to a farm that took us to the top of the valley. To reach this area, Tom, my hunting partner had a tractor and trailer parked in a shed and we swapped over the car for them as we were never going to make it into the top of the valley without the tractor. The road in was mud a lot of the time and the gear and I would travel in the trailer, the dogs would run along side as we weren't travelling very fast.

The outer farm boundary ran back into crown land, which is owned by the government, a massive area of hills and valleys covered in bush; many of them ran back to the Wanganui River, which ambled its way back to the town of Wanganui and then out to sea. The early settlers opened up many of the valleys to run sheep and cattle and were serviced by a paddle steamboat. The paddleboat would pick up the wool bails and other things the farmers had left on jetties that they had built and the boat people would leave supplies for the farmers and their families. This proved unprofitable for the boat owners' who also serviced the small settlements along the river banks, so the farmers built roads like the one Tom and I had come in by. This again proved unworkable as the roads in the winter time, especially those that ran from the top of the hill country to the valley floors, would suffer from landslides! The farmers tried to keep the roads open but over a period of time gave up and walked off the land, leaving much of their livestock behind.

In the mid 1960's there were quite good numbers of wild

pigs and cattle about the place and I think there still is today, its such an inaccessible place, rugged and steep, though the valleys themselves are quite wide, with very little bush and scrub on them, a very picturesque place. A great place to hunt and camp! The partnership with Tom lasted for about three months and was going along okay. We would hunt pigs for a few days at a time, bring them out and sell or raffle them in pubs around Wanganui. We made better money raffling most of the pigs, which we cut into quarters after skinning them out first, then selling them to the wild game buyers. We would sell the skinny sows and big smelly boars to the meat buyers; the Europeans, mainly Germans, as they didn't seem to care too much what they ate, but the Kiwis (NZ) did, so we raffled the best ones! Unfortunately Tom and I fell out because I got drunk one night and ran into the side of his house with my Thames van. He wasn't too happy about this and asked me to leave. (I could never understand why he did that!)

I grabbed my gear, dogs and left, and decided to go and stay with my aunty and cousins in a place called Waverly on the west coast, not too far from Wanganui. I got a job thinning out pine trees in plantations on farmers' properties and later on in the Patea meat works so settled in okay. One night, as I sat alone at home in the lounge watching T.V, I started to watch an evangelist preacher named Billy Graham. He was doing a crusade in NZ at the time and as I continued to watch him speak, I was amazed with the power of his speaking ability. I kept watching but then decided to turn him off. I sat there for a while just thinking about what he had said, then I turned on the TV again. I did this two or three times, I couldn't make up my mind if I wanted to watch him or not. This preacher seemed to have something to say that was catching my attention. I eventually went to bed as I had to get up early for hunting or work the next morning. One night when I was laying in bed thinking about where things came from, evolution popped into my mind? I tried to get my head around this theory but it didn't seem to make any sense to me, I just couldn't understand how things could come from nothing, I was sure this wasn't the answer I was looking for. The Catholic Church didn't give me the answers I was looking for either, that's why I left it! So what was I looking for?

# 2

# Coming Into His Grace

One of my cousins who I was staying with decided to head over to Western Australia (WA) to see what it was like there. He wrote to us after a while, saying that there was a lot of work and that the mining was booming. In those days the mining companies built small towns to accommodate workers and their families. This was a great way to encourage men to work in the mining industry. I decided I wanted to give it a go so I headed over to WA; it was Easter 1969. I dropped into Sydney first for a week to stay with my brother Denis, who had already been living there for two years. Mum and Dad came also and paid for my trip over (good old Mum and Dad). Once we got to Perth, I would be living with my cousin Bill O'Connell but Mum and Dad were going to keep going as they were heading on a world tour.

Bill had been working on an outback cattle station for a few months to give it a go, but then came back to Perth and we both got lodgings at a very good boarding house in Victoria Park. Bill bought an old Ford station wagon so we could get around the place. We both found jobs with a construction company, who were building a holding yard for the Chrysler car company. It wasn't difficult to get a job because of the boom in the mining industry up the North West. The foreman I worked with was a Dutchman from Melbourne, who had come over with his family seeking opportunity in Perth. His name was Hank Gomans, a very likeable bloke and he knew his job well.

   Hank got along with all us boys and I was made leading hand. One afternoon I walked into Hank's office and overheard him talking to one of the guys about Jesus. He was reading scripture out of his small bible. I had seen him reading his bible a few times before and wondered what it was all about. Hank and I started to talk about the things of God and he explained to me he had gotten out of the Catholic Church because he couldn't find the answers he was looking for. I related to this also because of my past experiences. After a while we became friends and Hank introduced me to his family; he had two attractive daughters about my age at the time and a son who was a bit younger. His wife was a very friendly person and they were a very hospitable bunch. They were all churchgoers and attended the Four Square Church; they invited me along one time so I decided to join them.

   The service was definitely different to the Catholic Church that I grew up in; it was a lot brighter, friendlier and a lot more appealing than what I was used to. It made me start to think about God and Jesus; I began to feel a lot more content. However knowing about God doesn't mean you know God on a personal level. I hadn't made that commitment of inviting Jesus into my life yet. I was lying in bed one night; Bill was asleep in a bed just across from me. I couldn't sleep so I lay meditating on the events that happened over the last couple of months. I suddenly blurted out "God, what ever Hank's got I want!"

It felt as though the whole room was illuminated with God's presence; there wasn't a light as such but it was His presence and I just knew it was Jesus. Tears started to cascade down my cheeks and the only word I could say was, "Jesus, Jesus, Jesus". I sprang out of bed and got dressed, all the time expecting my cousin to wake up, but he didn't. I got into my car and went to Hank's place about eight kilometres away. As I drove every traffic-light was green, wow, I don't know if it was God or coincidental but I was glad because I was a blubbering mess. Finally, I arrived at the Gomans' place and knocked on the door excited to see them. When they opened up for me, they knew God had come into my life and they invited me into their home. We got down on our knees and worshipped God. It is something that I have never forgotten even after forty odd years; the memory of that night is still so fresh today. I had finally found what I was looking for. I was born again by God's Holy Spirit. Scripture says in John 3:6 "I tell you the truth. No-one can see the kingdom of God unless he is born again". I had seen the Kingdom of God. I had found Jesus! God had saved me and now he wanted to kill me. As I go on in the book, I hope you will understand what I mean by that. Being a young Christian and coming into the saving knowledge of Jesus Christ, I wanted to tell everyone about Him. I was very zealous but with very little knowledge (of God and his way) or wisdom (could not keep my mouth shut about telling people about Jesus)!

# 3

# Growing Up in Him

When apostle Paul first got saved, he was very zealous; mind you, he had great intellectual knowledge of the Old Testament. Over time, God used this to bring him into an understanding of the New Testament church and what it was all about, but at the beginning of his ministry God had to restrain him! I had come into God's church, not a denomination, sect or group; not a religion but His church through Jesus Christ, our Lord and Saviour. I was a baby Christian and Jesus wanted me to grow up and mature me into whatever he had in mind for me. Jesus said He would build His church, not man, but He Himself would do it. Unfortunately we humans have tried to help out along the way far too much and like everyone that comes into His kingdom I had to learn this, it seems, the hard way.

The church is built on Christ Jesus (the corner stone), the apostles and the prophets and only through them will we come into the place of seeing His church built. What apostles and prophets some may ask? I believe the ones that helped write the Word of God, the Old and New Testaments. Not by our own endeavours, our might or our power but by His spirit will the church be built? To do this God has to kill our ego, so only Jesus will be high and lifted up, not us! When Jesus was heading up to the feast of Passover at Jerusalem, I believe that the enormity of what he had to go through to save mankind really sank in. He was contemplating asking God to save Him from that terrible event. He said "No, It was for this very reason I came to this hour. Father Glorify your name "John 12:27. Jesus was looking forward to God being glorified here on earth in the same way He was in heaven.

The Bible goes on to say; then a voice came from Heaven and said, "I have glorified it and will glorify it again". Through Jesus' death and resurrection, the Father was glorified and I believe that through the church he will be glorified again, but only through those that are willing to pay the price, the way of the cross. He will be glorified, and like Jesus there must be the work of the cross in our lives first. "Take up your cross and follow me." Jesus goes on to say in John 12:32 (NIV) "But when I am amplified up from the earth I will draw all men unto myself."

I believe the same applies to the church. I had come out of a tradition of religious instruction and I thought I was in the right church. Allow me to explain that; firstly coming out of the Catholic Church which had preached Jesus, but so much of their dogma and ritual got in the way, but later on down the track I still found the Lord, I believed they had helped me to do that. God was taking me on out of the frying pan into the fire, into the Pentecostal or charismatic movement. God wanted me to grow up for what He had in mind for me and at the same time moulding me along the way. There is no doubt about it, the speaking in tongues, prophesying, clapping of hands; bright singing, healing, praise and worship that I had come into was far more appealing to me than the structure I had experienced growing up. I was over the moon. After all those years of being taught a seemingly dead religion from the Catholic Church I felt like I wanted to blow up every building that looked like a church. Why hadn't the Catholic Church given me what I now had?" I didn't understand that God was setting my feet on a path to teach me His ways and to bring me into a relationship with Him. This can only be found through the cross; there is no other way. Jesus said if you want to reign with Him, you must also suffer with Him. It's not easy at times. Jesus asked the Father to take away the cross, and so will we; however, it was the glory that was before Jesus that kept Him going, and so it will be with us!

# 4

# Allowing God to Do It the Right Way

1 John 1:10 (NIV) "If we claim to be without sin we deceive ourselves and the truth is not in us." The Bible also says that the heart is the most deceitful and wicked above all things, Jeremiah 17:9. God had saved me; now He was about to show me what was in my heart. The church, or the bride of Christ, must be built or prepared by God through His spirit, His word and work of the cross. There is no other way, but as I said before, we humans want to help out along the way and I guess a lot of our motives have not always been too pure. We in Australia and I guess the Western world, govern things a certain way; for example, it is asserted a man is successful because he's achieved a lot of material goods by his own endeavours.

Working in itself is not wrong, in fact the bible teaches us to work hard at a living and other things we do. This success syndrome can be deceiving because some people don't want to achieve much of the world's goods and quite happy with what they have; quite possibly they have other priorities. The world and unfortunately the church, in some measure have used this so called 'success' as a yard stick of how to look at a person's character.

Unfortunately many self made people think that they don't need God. That's why Jesus said he came for the sick and not the well; really, he was having a shot at the self righteous. People that thought they could do God's work without him or without going through the cross first! King David was a man after God's heart. He was a boy looking after his father's sheep; he would bring God's presence by playing his harp and sing songs to the Lord. He would sit and meditate on the things of God. This would help him to become strong enough to overcome the bears and the lions that would try to take his father's sheep. Even though his life was mundane by being a shepherd boy, he was obedient to his calling. When the time came for him to overcome Goliath, who was scaring the hell out of Israel with all their might and armour, David overcame Goliath because he knew his God. (They that know their God shall do exploits). He had spent time with his God and entered into the presence of God.

Coming out of the Catholic Church into a Pentecostal church, I felt the presence of God in a way that I never had before and I loved it. God inhabits the praises of His people and God loves praise and worship; He manifests himself by His presence when the people of God sing and worship, I thought it was great.

I heard a preacher say one time that what the church needed was more ministries like such and such. Many of these folks have been used by God in a very real way and God blessed them for it. But I believe God is taking us into a deeper way of doing His will. Jesus said that the Father is looking for true worshipers in the spirit and in truth not just a few good ministries in our generation. God is restoring that which has been lost. He is bringing back true worshipers; people that will bring in His presence, and do his will the right way.

King David loved God's presence as do many of God's people today. They long to see God glorified in His church, to see Jesus high and lifted up so that the world will be drawn to Him. There is a right way and there is a wrong way to do this and God wants to show us His way. As I said King David loved God's presence but the church of that time had lost touch with God's presence to the world. In those days God's presence was on a box called the Ark of the Covenant and God chose to manifest himself on that box. David understood how to bring God's presence for himself, but also above all, to have it back in Israel. 1 Samuel 4:1-11 (NIV) tells us how Israel lost the glory of Israel, the presence of God. 1 Samuel 4:19-22 9 (NIV) "The glory has departed from Israel for the Ark of God has been captured and it was called Ichabod". (The glory has departed).

Today we think that we have God's presence in fullness in our churches, but much is still captured by the world. We the church have tried to bring in God's presence by the way of the world, and it has bought many under bondage but God is about to set the captives free by teaching us his ways, the right way. We in the church have tried to build God a temple and bring in his presence by much of our own endeavours. I believe God is saying "Enough, enough, I will do it my way", God is putting the axe to the root of the tree and that which is of the flesh will be burnt up. I believe God is bringing forth a revelation of what His true church is all about, as we in the church have tried on many occasions to bring in his glory by the wrong way! God is looking for the heart of obedience not endeavours of super men. Since I became a Christian I have seen so many men of God fall (were they men of God, sometimes it makes you wonder). So many endeavours come to nought, so much wasted money and so many Christian's burn and fall away. People that still love the Lord but will not go back to church unless God intervenes and I believe He will. We will see God restoring his church as we get out of the way and allow Jesus to do it, he said he would and it will happen. What we need is ears to hear what the spirit is saying to the churches. To do what is needed, we must take time out, stop all the huff and puff, sweat of the brow and all the rubbish we call church and allow God to show us His way.

The Ark of God had been lost to the world until David was made King. King David loved God and loved His presence, and he wanted the glory back to its rightful place. 2 Samuel 6 (NIV) - Restores the Ark of God - the glory of the Lord had been captured by the Philistines (the flesh, the system of the world) but they found they couldn't handle it because the Lord had sent a sickness through their camp 1 Samuel 5:6 (NIV) so the Philistines, sent it back.

When I look back over the years from 1969 when I first came to know the Lord and the things that have gone on in the church with leadership errors, I can understand why so many people have not gone back to church! Not long after I got saved, I went to an outreach meeting in a church that was in an old theatre; the preacher was a Kiwi (NZ) evangelist and pastor from not too far away from where I came from in New Zealand. He had been invited over to take some meetings. In fact, some of my mates back in NZ had been saved through his ministry. It was a happy-clappy type of service which I found great, after the Catholic Church. People would go to the front when he finished his preaching and he would pray for them. There was only one sermon that I remember when he spoke on tithing and was adamant that you tithe before your tax was taken out. I remember feeling disturbed by this type of message as the church I came out from was full of rules and regulations (legalism). Coming to know Jesus I felt such a freedom, this message being preached seemed a contradiction from what I had come into.

Being a new Christian and not knowing any better, I more or less accepted this as fact, I wanted to follow Jesus, but something didn't sit right with my spirit. I started to attend this church and the people were friendly to me, which helped me with my walk with the Lord. We would meet down in the theatre until that became unavailable and then we started to meet upstairs in a smaller area. The church was run by two pastors; one was a great evangelist and the other a great teacher. I grew to admire these guys over a period of time as they helped me grow spiritually and there was a great balance. The next chapter explains this in more detail.

# 5

# Presumption in the Church

Presumption is something that seems to be rife in the church of Jesus Christ. 1 Samuel 4 (NIV) right through the whole chapter teaches us that the Philistines captured the Ark of God because the Israelites did not seek the Lord for guidance regarding a battle that they were involved in. It was not going very well for them. 1 Samuel 4:3 (NIV) says when the soldiers returned to camp (after the first battle), the elders of Israel asked (not God), "Why did the Lord bring defeat upon us today before the Philistines? Let us (presuming that God would bless this move) bring the Ark of the Lords covenant from Shiloh so that it may go well with us and save us from the hand of our enemies". Verse 4 tells that even Hophni and Phinehas, the sons of Eli the high priest, who were the priests looking after the Ark of God, went along with the move to do this thing. Verse 5 lets us know that the people of Israel thought it was okay as well and they let out such a great shout that even the ground shook. It all seemed to be so good and proper that it had to be of God. Of course it was but it wasn't! Let's see what happened in verse 10. The Philistines fought and the Israelites were defeated and every man fled to his tent. The slaughter was very great. Israel lost 30,000 foot soldiers. Verse 11 the Ark of God was captured and Eli's two sons, Hophni and Phinehas died. The people of Israel presumed that by taking the Ark of the Lord with them into battle that possibly they shouldn't have been involved in at that time or even if they were, the fact was it was just a religious act. The Ark of the Lord was at that time was to be kept in a tent at Shiloh, which it was, until it was wrongfully taken out and then captured by the world (Philistines). The elders should have sought the Lord on their knees, not worked on presumption that having the ark with them would have help their cause and win the battle. Because the Lord wasn't blessing this thing they did, it cost a lot of lives and they lost the very presence of the Lord in Israel of the day to the world!

Since I have been a Christian I have seen and been involved with this type of thing. I guess we all have somewhere along the way, but for some reason we don't seem to learn, it is the heart thing again. Jeremiah 17:9&10 (RSV). The heart is deceitful above all things and desperately corrupt, who can understand it? Verse 10 says I, the Lord search the mind and try the heart to give to every man according to his ways, according to the fruit of his doings. The Bible says that a man of God is led by the spirit of God; to be led we must first try the spirit to see where it comes from. Things might seem good and holy and we feel we have the Lord's approval on it – but things can be so off and it can bring nothing but death, destruction and captivity.

Test it, test it and test it again, God doesn't mind because if it's okay He will bring in such a liberty of knowing, that we know that it's from Him. God tells us to test the spirit because where the Spirit of Jesus is there's freedom not bondage. Not just to presume that everything that we feel is of God. We must be lead by His word, testing it out by two or three witnesses, allowing the peace of God to be our guide. Some things we have to allow God to show us our hearts or motives of why we want to rush off and do things without checking them out first. Jesus did what the Father showed Him and He learned to be obedient to it. He was delighted to do God's will!

One of the pastors that had been a farmer was called to preach and thought that God had told him to sell his farm, move to Western Australia, start a church and Bible school. (We call them mega churches today). The idea was to buy land, subdivide it, sell it for a profit and use the money to build a church and bible school. People put a lot of money into the project, from which they would receive a financial gain if all went to plan, all for the glory of God or so we like to say. (I wonder what the heart is really saying) maybe it is saying something like this; 'A quick buck and it will work because it's from God, the pastor said it's from God, so it must be!' The other pastor came in on the scheme as another senior pastor. If I had joined the church when this thing was started, I might have put money into it as well but I didn't. I joined when the boat was being rocked, and things were being blown apart. A lot of people, God's people, lost a lot of money because of presumption, thinking that God would hold this thing up but He didn't. Jeremiah 17:4 (NIV) 'Through your own fault you will lose the inheritance that I gave you'. People were devastated and as a young Christian so was I. How could God allow these things to happen to His people? The Bible says;

'Commit your ways to the Lord and He will guide your paths'. I believe that there were a lot of bad business dealings, not dishonest, but they just didn't really know what they were doing at the time. How often do we see things like this happen in the church? Jesus says to check out the cost first, not presume on God. Over the years I have become quite cynical about a lot of so called things of God. When we realise that the church is not a building then we might be on the right track. Why is it that we seem to think success in the things of God is always about big and more? It is because this is the way that the world thinks, because big is best and more is a sign of success. For me to say that God wasn't in the foundation of this particular church would be silly. I had come into a family and they were looking after me, even though there were mistakes along the way and this event was only the start of it!

There was a man in the good old USA that built big buildings, campuses and a university. He would say he was one of the most famous preachers after Billy Graham. He was always after money like so many of these blokes and their schemes that they say God has told them to build. One time he said that God would take his life if he didn't get eight million dollars ($8,000,000), not knowing better I got sucked in and sent in money. I didn't ask the Lord first, thinking I was helping but wasn't. As far as I can make out, his projects had been taken over by secular administration and they were about $52,000,000 US in debt, that man was Oral Roberts. According to what I have read, Roberts and his wife came from a background where their fathers were preachers on the fringes of the Pentecostal movement. In that church to be a Christian, one needed to be poor. Mrs Roberts and her husband, Oral, yearned respectability and they resented poverty. Oral Roberts' so called liberation from this type of thing came as he read 3 John 2 and also had an audible message from God. (I really don't believe he heard from the true God). I believe he and his organisation had run with this so called prosperity gospel. (Deceiving and being deceived). Roberts wrote a small booklet about how to "Get out of dept supernaturally" shame he didn't live it. I believe he and many like him have done the church a disservice by running ahead with God's word, not checking out their so called written and audible messages from God. I believe its false doctrine but many believe it because it appeals to the flesh; again, which god did they hear from. What's really in their heart? Big and rich is right! Poverty is so wrong.

Hey look at Job who went through poverty for a season. He lost everything except his wife! But because his attitude was right before God he came into a greater relationship of knowing his God. Even though he had a lot and then lost it all, he still blessed the Lord. The Lord meant more to Job than all his riches and being respectable, which in itself can be a trap by allowing man to govern us and quite often we have to keep up with the Joneses to fulfil the ambitions of it. The Bible says don't govern someone by the abundance of the things he has! The Bible also says that God will supply all our needs, not our lusts. Job lost everything and his so called friends said he was in some sin for this to happen! Job knew better but this in itself made it harder for him to understand why he was going through this trial; he knew he was right before God. When the trial was finally over the Lord restored back to Job double what he had lost. God knew

Job's heart and he knew that Job didn't worship him because of the abundance of the things he allowed him to have, but that Job worshiped God because he wanted to! The riches that God allowed Job to have were secondary to his relationship with his God. We have to be so careful which god controls us. If we are being driven to do God's will, check it out, because as I have come to realise, the true Shepherd leads! We follow Him and are not driven by the desires of the flesh. I believe that the Bible Roberts got his so called instruction from for his prosperity gospel was the King James version 3 John 2 (KJV) "I wish above all things that thou mayest prosper and be in health, even as thy soul prospereth". Hey, it's in the Bible and it's the King James Version so it must be right! The Bible also says in 2 Timothy 2:15 (NIV) "Do your best to present yourself to God as one approved, a workman who does not need to be ashamed and who correctly handles the word of truth" also the King James version "Study to show thyself approved unto God, a workman that needeth not to be ashamed, rightly dividing the word of truth."

The King James Version is not wrong but the word prospers if taken out of context; it can and does lead many astray, especially if it appeals to the flesh, or in other words our lusts! The NIV study bible, 3 John 2 "Dear friends, I pray that you may enjoy good health and that all will go well with you, even as your soul is getting along well". In the context in which it was written, it has nothing to do with being or getting rich; read the whole thing yourself. Let's have look at the Revised Standard Version 3 John 2 "Beloved I pray that all may go well with you and that you maybe in health, I know that is well with your soul!" It's nothing more than what we often ask or say to our friends! Sometimes they could say back to us, "Yes great, good job, good money coming in and feeling as fit as a buck rabbit!" Other times they could say something like this, "I wish things could be a little better, lost my job, bills up to my eyeballs and the Mrs is as sick as a dog!" And then we could self-righteously say to them: "Where's your faith bro?" To make them feel better of course! Again, nothing to do with God making us richer or always been in health. See the Writer had a desire that these things are with his friend. He wished above all things that it was so, but God could have had other ideas. Thicker than two planks are these prosperity preachers and yet their doctrine has run amok in much of the church. 2 Jeremiah 17:10-11 says 'When I the Lord searches the heart and examines the mind to reward man according to his conduct, according to what his deeds deserve. Like a partridge that hatches eggs that it did not lay is the man that gains riches by unjust means, when his life is half gone, they will desert him and in the end he will prove to be a fool'. How many so called men of God (I thought a man of God is led by the spirit of God) have crashed and burned. Their so called God projects have gone and they are left with egg on their faces.

Believe me I am not writing this lightly. It took forty odd years of being involved in the church and with the fear of God on me (he's my dad) to write this. God will not be mocked and He will be glorified in His church. All we have to do is keep on track, hear what He is saying, repent if we make a blue and fall back into line because He loves us. If this type of thing happened again, and someone asked me for money and said God would kill them if they didn't get such and such an amount by a certain time, I possibly would say something like this: "Die then, because at least then you will be with the Lord (I hope) but not down here deceiving people to part with their money to build your kingdom". Good question. What Kingdom are we building?

# 6

# Who is Building the Church?

We the church must come to a place of realising that He is building His church not us. What we have to do is seek first the kingdom of God and His righteousness and we are a part of what he is doing. It is not man that builds the church - but God. Jeremiah 17:5 (NIV) says this is what the Lord says so we had better listen: 'Cursed is the one who trusts in man, who depends on flesh of His strength and whose heart turns away from the Lord'. "WE CAN'T SERVE TWO MASTERS". These prosperity preachers seem to think you can! Who do we believe them or Our Lord? When we try to build the church on our own strength, abilities and money we fail! God Himself will blow on it and it will fail. It might have all the outward appearances of Godliness but denies the power of God to deal with the heart. We the kids of God must learn to see and understand the differences. Now we realise that a lot of good things have been done in the church, everywhere, but for some reason we seem to overlook the past mistakes, thinking it won't happen to us. This is a lie, Jesus warned us that deception would be rife in the last days; we must gird our hearts because we can be so easily led astray.

Genesis 3:1 (NIV) 'Now the serpent was craftier than any of the wild animals that the Lord God had made. Revelation 12:9-20 (NIV) the devil or Satan is referred to as 'that ancient serpent'. Wow, God had made serpents or snakes so they were okay. But Satan, the great deceiver, had clothed himself as a serpent; maybe snakes could talk in that day. They do to today, deceiving and being deceived. What's the old saying? "A snake in the grass", someone to watch out for! He (the serpent) said to the woman (the one that man should have been protecting), did God really say, sowing doubt in her mind and appealing to her lust? Adam and Eve were created with a free will to choose between right and wrong. God had given them everything they needed. Paul said to be content with raiment and food. It doesn't mean that God can't give us more. In His timing, Eve saw what God had forbidden was good for food and looked good, so she wanted it. She wanted to be like God knowing good and evil, but up until that time they were innocent. It didn't matter if it was Adam or Eve or someone else, we would have all failed the test. It is in our hearts; we all have freewill and choose to go the way of sin. Thank God for Jesus and what He did on the cross, for if we sin today all we have to do is repent and allow God to take us on. We don't have to go through the rigmarole of the law to please God. The law was really brought in to show us how bad a sinner we are, how Holy God is and that we aren't going to make it by our endeavours anyway. Paul said "we see through a glass darkly", what it means is that we understand God, Jesus and His kingdom only with a limited knowledge but one day we will understand fully, God has given us enough to go on to bring us to that place.

Paul said "That I might know Him (not know about Him) and the power of His resurrection".

Going on with God, our church family was about to go through a spiritual divorce which would rock me more than even the money matters we had gone through before. The board and one of the pastors had decided that the other pastor wasn't quite with the program or vision, and asked him to leave. As a young Christian I was devastated because the pastor they were asking to leave had been a part of the ministry for some time and had helped me so much. Doesn't the Bible say we are built up through spiritual gifts and ministry? We, the church, were a family being torn apart because one of the oversights was asked to go. It possibly felt like a divorce, where one person wanted it, but the other didn't! As I have gone on in the Lord over the years I have noticed some things with divorce, I'm talking about the people whose agenda wants a divorce.

I lost my beautiful wife just over seven years ago to cancer and being married for thirty seven years I know that marriage is not a bed of roses; it can be really hard work at times. Quite often when there is a split in the church or a marriage, the motives are wrong, things that could have been worked out in God are not. Quite often, the one who wants the split doesn't really seek the Lord with a pure heart. When a man and woman get married, they really are saying I surrender to you even though we are quite different in some ways and our personalities are not really alike but I have committed myself to you even though it's going to go against the grain at the time. It means I have to let go of my own ambitions and my own wants, for the good of the marriage and the family. It doesn't mean I don't have desires and dreams but they must fit in with you for we are one.

I found that not too long after I was married that I needed God to bring me to that place more and more as we went on in our marriage. I found myself asking God to make me a better husband, not Rosemary a better wife. When ministers start working with others, the same as in business or marriage, they are going into a partnership with other personalities, different ways of doing things, different likes and dislikes. At times things can be rocky but that doesn't mean we give up, especially if other children are involved. I didn't really care what the church plans were, what they had in mind or vision; all I knew was that due to a different agenda by one of the pastors my spiritual oversight was parting and as a child in God I was devastated, just as well God kept me from knowing there was worse to come. In the natural order I found that kids don't really care about how much money their parents have, how big their house is or about their folk's plans for the future. All they really want is love. Because we live in a society that seems to be driven by these other things, to the degree it's become sickly, like eating too much honey. In many of the churches, we have allowed the system of the world to rule and I feel we are blind too much of it. Lust of the flesh, pride of life, must keep up with the Jones', bigger and richer is best - all in the name of the Lord. Is it God's will be done; I would say some of it is a no. When I first came to the Lord just after Easter in 1969, God had being doing a thing and was bringing hundreds of thousands of people to him, especially young people. I remember reading about this in Time and Life magazines which had dedicated the main story to what was happening in the USA. They had page after page with photos and stories of what was going on. They called it the Jesus Revolution and the people involved Jesus People. I didn't really know what it was all about, but one of my pastors whom I was speaking to about it thought it was great. The movement of the Holy Spirit was sweeping through many of the western countries and was changing much of the culture of the church.

It was the time of the Vietnam war, many people were opposed to the status quo of the day and another movement had started called the hippie movement, where younger people started living in communes and free love, drugs and rock and roll were the order of the day. Alternative religions from the eastern culture were also tried. The church had failed them and they were looking for answers. Many of the top bands and singers of the time got involved one way or another. There was a spiritual hunger that only God could fill; and he was doing it, but much of it not through the established church. God started doing this by bringing people who were hungry and thirsty for righteousness, whose motives were pure. 'Blessed are the pure in heart for they will see God', Matthew 5:8.

God was rising up people who only wanted to serve God, who didn't have any other agenda, but a people that were not interested in starting churches, about how much money they could make out of the gospel, about being big time but only serving God. God started to use them to change much of the direction of the church. The Jesus revolution which was sweeping among young people and I happened to be one of them, it was a massive move of God. At the same time there was a revival in the churches which was called the charismatic renewal. God was restoring in the church spiritual gifts, God didn't give the gifts as a joke. Paul in 1 Corinthians 12:15 (NIV) tell us why they are given. The apostle Paul knew how important they were but he also knew how to use them the right way in the church and for his own building up. Chapter 14:18 (NIV) 'I thank God that I speak in tongues more than all of you'. The whole idea of speaking in tongues personally was for building up our own spirit. Allowing God through the Holy Spirit to do it for us, bypassing our intellect, it is for edification of oneself and the church, chapter 14:4. At the end of the day or the charismatic renewal was tongues and I can see why Jesus himself said 'Those who believe will speak in new tongues' Mark 16:17 (NIV) I want to make it quite clear that the gifts of the Holy Spirit do not save - Jesus does. The night I got saved it was Jesus. I kept saying Jesus not tongues or any other gift. The gift I got was salvation from my sins and I became a child of the living God. I was part of His family as we all are who believe. There is no different from one who speaks in tongues and one who does not. We are all His kids. As I said God didn't give the gifts of the Holy Spirit for a joke but to take the church on to make Jesus more real to the world through them. The gifts were given for the edification of oneself and the church (building up). It was at that time that God showed me that there were many Catholics that really loved the Lord and were seeking a deeper walk with Him. It was quite a time and eye opener to me. There's a saying that I pinched of someone else, "To know about God, does not really know God!" Jesus said that the Pharisees had knowledge of the scriptures but didn't know him. It should always be our aim to know him more and the only way is death to self and obedience to His calling in our lives. Romans 8:17 (NIV) 'Now if we are children then we are heirs - heirs of God and co-heirs with Christ. If indeed we share His suffering in order that we may also share in His Glory.' God wants to bring His Glory back to the church and just like Israel the church has lost it in many areas. As I said before there's a right way and there's a wrong way of bringing in His glory.

# 7

# Bring Back God's Glory The Right Way

King David saw an opportunity to bring the glory of God back to its rightful place. On his first attempt it failed and cost a man his life in 2 Samuel 6:1-7 (NIV). David again brought together out of Israel (chosen men, thirty thousand in all). He and all his men set out from Baalah of Judah to bring up from there the Ark of God, which is called by the name, the name of the Lord Almighty who is enthroned between the cherubim that are on the ark, they set the Ark of God on a new cart. (The Philistines used a new cart which speaks of the way of the world, not God's way. Pride of life, lust of the flesh, system of the world etc!) Unfortunately King David got sucked in by this method and bought it from the house of Abinadab, which was on the hill. Uzzah and Ahio, sons of Abinadab were guiding the new cart with the Ark of God on it and Ahio was walking in the front of it. David and the whole house of Israel were celebrating with all their might before the Lord, with songs, harps, lyres, tambourines, sistrums and cymbals. When they came to the threshing floor of Nachon, Uzzah reached out and took hold of the Ark of God because the oxen stumbled. The Lords anger burned against Uzzah because of this irreverent act. Verse 8 Therefore God struck him down and he died beside the Ark of God. Let's hold it there a bit - The threshing floor is a place where the chaff gets sorted out from the wheat, a place of separation and judgement.

Mathew 3:11 (NIV) John the Baptist speaking about Jesus - 'I baptise you with water for repentance but after me will come one who is more powerful than I, whose sandals I am not fit to carry. He will baptise you with the Holy Spirit and with fire. Verse 12 His winnowing fork is in his hand and he will clear His threshing floor, gathering his wheat into the barn and burning up the chaff with unquenchable fire'. When the cart came to the threshing floor God said enough is enough and started to rock the boat (cart). Uzzah tried to stop it and he died because of it. God will bring judgement on the church to clean out the chaff, that which is of the flesh and the works of man. He will rock the cart, the new cart, to get our attention because we are in many cases not bringing in the glory of God the right way. This will upset many people because they think they are doing the will of God. David thought He was doing God's will the right way by bringing the Ark of God back to its rightful place by a cart (the way of the world) and God said 'No, wrong way'. David presumed he was doing it the right way but he should have known better. 2 Samuel 6:8 David was angry because the Lord's wrath had broken out against Uzzah and to this day that place is called Perez Uzzah (it was a divine warning for us to take note that Uzzah had tried to stop God's ways. God was judging David and the people by rocking the cart and Uzzah in his humanistic way tried to stop God and it cost him his life). Flesh and blood will not inherit the kingdom of heaven. Flesh and blood will never bring in the glory of God, for this to happen the flesh must die. God's way not our ways, so we may as well get used to it. It is through much trials and tribulation that we enter into the kingdom of heaven Acts 14:22 (RSV).

Mark 8:32&33 (NIV) teaches that Peter had a similar problem to Uzzah; he wanted to stop Jesus from going to the cross and Jesus in verse 33 rebuked Peter and called him Satan. The flesh will always take the easy way to bring God's glory in. 2 Samuel 6:9-14 (NIV) David was afraid of the Lord that day and said 'How can the Ark of the Lord ever come to me?' This got David seeking the Lord for the right way of bringing back the glory of the Lord. Verse 12 King David was told 'the Lord has blessed the household of Obed-Edom and everything he has because of the Ark of God. David had left it there after he was rebuked at the threshing floor. David went and bought up the Ark of God from the house of Obed-Edom to the city of David with rejoicing. Verse 13 When those who were carrying the Ark of the Lord had taken six steps, the right way to bring in the glory was on the shoulders of the priesthood not on carts, the flesh and the way of the world. We are all priests and kings from the least to the greatest in the church and if we want to become the greatest we have to become the least and there is only one way for that to happen. The cross, death to self and death to our ambitions, death to our own agendas, death to how we will build God's church, allowing God to give us a new heart, a pure heart, then we will see God, and then we will allow his glory to shine from His church because we will be completely surrendered to him and bring back the glory the right way! Verse 14 David wearing a linen ephod danced before the

Lord with all his might. After David became offended because he didn't seek the Lord about how to bring the ark back the first time the right way, he inquired of God about how to do it the prescribed way. 1 Chronicles 15:13 (NIV) he realised the way he presumed to bring back the ark, and remember it hadn't been done for a long time, was not the way of the Lord and it was costing men their lives. There was only one way that was accepted by God in bringing His glory back. 1 Chronicles 15:11-15 (NIV) Then David summoned Zadok and Abiathar the priests and Uriel, Asaiah, Joel, Shemaiah, Eliel and Amminadab the Levites. Verse 12 He said to them 'You are the heads of the Levitical families', (mature leaders, people that understood God and His ways). Not just people with gifts but very little experience of life and God's ways. Like so many of the young people and others that are put in places of leadership today, you and your fellow Levites are to consecrate (to make oneself sacred- to prepare oneself) yourselves and bring up the Ark of the Lord, the God of Israel, to the place I have prepared for it. Verse 13, It was because you the Levites did not bring it up the first time the Lord our God broke out in anger against us. We did not enquire of Him about how to do it in the prescribed way (right way). David had tried to bring back the glory of God the first time by the way of the world (on a cart) BUT it will not be done with the might or power of men but by people and leaders that consecrate themselves in humility, that are willing to let go of self, their abilities and desires. Those that will allow God to mold them, crush them till that true priesthood is ready to bring back the presence of God. King David, a man after God's own heart, had to learn this the hard way but he did learn.

# 8

# Spending Time with God and His Word

We live in a society that sells a lot of stuff that has instructions on how to put it together but when you start to read much of these instructions it seems to be so much information. We tend to get overwhelmed by all of this so we toss them out and try to build the thing we had got our own way. Something that should have taken a lot less time to make takes hours and we have to go back to the instructions anyway. The church is so much like that, I guess its human nature, but God wants to kill that nature so the nature of His son Jesus comes through. God wants to break our will so that His will - will be done. God's way or no way! Letting go of self is not easy, we must reckon ourselves dead. The first mistake that King David did was not to ask God how His glory should be brought back to Israel the right way 1 Chronicles 15:5-15 (NIV) The second time he did! "And the Levites carried the Ark of God with the poles on their shoulders as Moses had commanded according with the word of the Lord, because we don't live under the law anymore it is still a type or shadow for us new saints to get instructions from. David had to go back and study the word and allow God to speak to him through it. Not run off and do his own thing because it felt right 2 Timothy 2:15 (KJV). 'Study to show thyself approved unto God, a workman that needed not be ashamed, rightly dividing the word of truth'. David had found truth, which set them free to bring the glory of God back to Israel the right way. When you study 2 Samuel 6:1-9 (NIV) It was the wrong way of bringing the Ark of God (his presence) then in 1 Chronicles 15:11-28 (NIV) and 2 Samuel 12:12-19 (NIV) the right way. They almost seem similar. There was singing and music and celebrating with all their might it seemed like a good Pentecostal church, dancing and shouting, they both had the lot. However one way brought death 2 Samuel 16:6&7 (NIV) and the other way brought life. The first way was done on presumption and not inquiring first from the Lord. The second was to seek God first and His righteousness. The first way was to use chosen men and they tried to use the way of the world (the cart), the flesh always tries the easy way but it brought death. The second way by consecrated men. Men and women set aside because they had allowed God to deal with their hearts, where they could say 'Not my will, but your will be done. I will do it your way Father God'. The second brought liberty and life.

God is rising up anointed teachers and prophets, people that have the word of the Lord, the word of revelation as Peter did when he said Jesus was the Son of God. He had a revelation of which Jesus was and Jesus said by this way He will build His church, the rock of revelation not by presumption because it feels and seems good. The church today needs a new fresh revelation of God's way but it must be consecrated unto the Lord. Under the Old Law the requirements of consecrating by the priests was through a ritual washing and avoidance of ceremonial defilement. Exodus 29:1-37, Exodus 30:19-21, Exodus 40:31&32 and Leviticus 8:5-35 (NIV) we need under the new covenant to get back to allowing God through his word and avoidance of things that hinder God from pouring out His glory. One thing that seems to be lacking in the church is maturity and this seems over the 20 to 25 years or so seems more and more that the church is run by young people and immature Christians. They may seem to have zeal and drive but lack wisdom and experience of life. Jesus himself was 30 years of age before he went out into His public ministry. He was a carpenter as was I. He knew how to work in the heat of the day with dirt on his hands, He knew how to put up with all the requirements that it took to do the job. Jesus as a Jew would have been brought up with a knowledge of the scriptures but He also worked for a living. Today young people and many new Christians go through bible college and then into youth ministry or music ministry as leaders. Even at times being made pastors to lead the church and they haven't got a real clue what life is all about. The world might do this but the church shouldn't. Paul in the New Testament said the leaders and deacons should know how to look after their own family first and would give them an insight as how to look after the church. We today need a maturity of experience and wisdom. People that have been through the mill of life, suffering when their kids go off track, somebody like the prodigal son, or a financial situation hits and they have to really trust God to get them through it, etc. The list goes on and on. Knowing about God doesn't mean we know God. There is a massive difference; we can't expect the church to grow into maturity if it's run by girls and boys. David was anointed to be king at a young age 1 Samuel 17:34-36 (NIV) and had great talent at many things but didn't become into the fullness of his kingship for many years after he was anointed by the prophet Samuel. He reigned over Judah for seven years and six months and then over all the other tribes for thirty three years, 40 years all up 2 Samuel chapters 5.(NIV) God put him through some great trials before he made him king over Israel. God used the hard times to mature David so he could rule with fairness and justice. 1 Chronicles 18:14 "David reigned over all Israel doing what was just and right for all his people". Saul brought bondage and slavery to the people when he was king, he was made king and started to rule straight away. The people wanted this type of king, not really knowing what they were letting themselves in for, not seeking the Lord first! God allowed this thing to happen to teach the people a lesson! 1 Samuel 8:4-8 (NIV) so all the elders of Israel (elders were the leaders of the people) gathered together and came to Samuel at Ramah. They said to him 'You are old and your sons do not walk in your ways, now appoint a king to lead us, such as all the other nations have'.

The people wanted a king like the nations of the world. How much does it seem to be like the church in the world today? So much ambition to build the house of God according to the pattern of the world. How much does it seem to be like the church in the West today? Big is successful, rich is right, so we judge according to what the world classes as right and yet God does not care about these things as He is more interested in the heart, God can give us these things if He so wills. We can ask for these things and what if he says 'NO', like he did with King David, when he wanted to build the temple for the ark to dwell in. What David was asking was not wrong, he had good intentions but God said no. 2 Samuel 7:5 (NIV) 'Go and tell my servant David this is what the Lord says - 'Are you the one to build me a house to dwell in?' Verse. 12 'When your days are over and you rest with your Father I will raise up your offspring to succeed you, who will come from your own body, and I will establish his kingdom (Solomon). Verse 13 "He is the one who will build a house for my name" God said 'NO' to David.

# 9

# When God says No, we need to hear it

Acts 16:6 (NIV) Paul and his companions travelled through out of the region of Phrygia and Galatia having been kept by the Holy Spirit from preaching the word in the province of Asia. Verse 7 'When they came to the border of Mysia, they tried to enter Bithynia but the Spirit of Jesus would not allow them to'. God in His wisdom says no at times to our requests and He does it because He knows better. We as humans often rush off to build God's kingdom or even our own without seeking God first to find out if it's okay by the Lord to do these things. James 3:17 (NIV) "Listen, you who say today or tomorrow we will go to this or that city, spend a year there, carry on business, make money, why: you do not even know what will happen tomorrow. What is your life? You are a mist that appears for a little while and then vanishes. Verse 15 Instead you ought to say, "if it is the Lord's will, we will live and do this or that, this boasting and bragging is evil". So we must in the church and our lives find out what the will of God is. Sometimes it is hard and we won't like it but we must let the peace of God rule in our hearts, this is the greatest guide we have, test the spirit and allow peace to rule in our lives.

King David in fact, if you study scripture, you will find that anybody who really did the will of God went through hard times but it got them to a place that God could use them, they knew God not just knew about Him. Ambitions of the heart, ego, etc are some of the signs we have to watch out for. The bible says 'Out of the overflow of the heart the mouth speaks' Matthew 12:34.(NIV) Have you ever noticed that sometimes we ask how a person is or how things are going and at the beginning of the conversation everything seems fine but along the way what's really in their hearts comes flowing out. When you wade through all that they say, things are not as good as they made out to be in the beginning. You really only have to listen to a person for a while and you will start to find out what's really in their hearts. What concerns me is the way the churches are built. Not necessarily the material construction but the way or motive for why it was built. I know it's for the glory of God, of course it is, or is it? (Is it for self glory?). Maybe you think I am a little sceptical with my approach on this matter, I have become a little bit more careful on how I judge things for sure. All the years of being with the Lord has taught me that. At the same time when I have seen the same stuff ups time and time again I often wonder where the church is going. It's like ground hog day, same old, same old. Music might have changed a bit, slightly different style but as long as it brings in the presence of God and gives honour to Him, it doesn't really matter. There is some really great music done by Christians today, some really get into your spirit and you can feel God in it! Then there is other stuff that only touches the selfish parts of us, done from the carnal mind. We are told not to operate the church according to the pattern of the world. I will give some examples of what I mean.

Firstly the church is a family and we are to look out for one another, especially the leadership, pastors who should have a shepherd heart, looking out for the sheep because Satan is so cunning and our hearts so evil we need continuously to watch out for them and be on guard. The first Christians suffered terrible persecution under the Roman rule and also by the Jews. Some lost their property and some even lost their lives because they believed in Jesus. Today in our Western countries this is not so, in some other countries yes but not in the West. I believe that when we have outward persecution, people can see this and will often build up to a resolve that will overcome it. Because of the marketing society we live in today, the church has come under attack in a way that is very under handed and very dangerous. We live in a society that plays on our senses. Absolutes are not absolute anymore, a spade is not a spade anymore, it's an agricultural implement. We don't marry anymore; have a husband and a wife, we have a partner. It's now okay if the same sex partners live together; it's all okay because they love one another. They are not called homosexuals or sodomites any more; they are called gay. (When I think about it, I cannot for the life of me see anything gay about being a homosexual). By watering down words like homosexual or sodomite and calling it gay makes it feel acceptable. Let's see what the bible says about truth and glorifying God. Paul's writing to the Roman Christians in Romans 1:21 (NIV) "For although they knew God, they neither glorified Him as God nor gave thanks to Him, their foolish hearts were darkened". We live in a society that once, in some ways, glorified God by our laws and by many of His values, but little by little much of it is being eroded away and I wonder is it because we the church have lost much of its influence to maintain these values? Verse 22 although they claimed to be wise, they became fools and exchanged the glory of the immortal God for images made to look like a mortal man and birds and animals and reptiles. Centuries before and after the writing of this letter to the Roman Christians, man made images of man and beasts were worshiped by them. Act 19:23 (NIV) "About that time there occurred no small disturbance concerning the way (the church at Ephesus) for a man names Demetrius, a silversmith who made silver shrines of Artemis. "Not only is there danger that this trade of ours fall into disrepute, but also that the temple of the great goddess Artemis be regarded as worthless and she whom all of Asia and the world worship will even be dethroned from her magnificence." The gospel had made so much in roads in Ephesus that the people were not buying shrines made to their god and this upset the tradesmen that made them, because they could have gone broke and lost their trade. Man seems to love to worship every thing else but the living God. God above all is looking for true worshipers in the spirit and in truth. Society says if it feels good then do it. We have been lead to believe we are lead by our feelings. The bible says we are to be lead by the Spirit of God who in turn uses the word of God to help us understand His ways so we can worship the right way.

Deception is one of our greatest enemies, as I have said before, as a younger Christian I had seen and been through some bad stuff in the church I was attending, they were my family. After things settled down from the pastor being thrown out of the church, it seemed we were getting back on track. I loved the Lord, all I wanted was to go on with him and know I was really hungry for the things of God. As I said it seemed like we were getting back on track and good things were happening. I still missed the other pastor, he had made a big input into my life and I felt something was missing. We started to meet with another church that was run by a woman. Those days there were not too many Pentecostal churches around and together we had some good services. We would meet in a large hall but after a while we stopped meetings together for a season. The ladies church had brought a large block of land to build a church on, but before this took place and while we were still meeting together, the two churches invited another minister from Queensland to come and share. The way the minister spoke looked more like a performance to me. This is one of the reasons I have called this book "Oh Church, why so Much Like a Circus?", it just didn't feel right and there was so much performance. That minister of the gospel liked the girls and after two or three bad moves on his part, was asked to step down as he was a married man. How much of God's work is built up by the flesh. Only what God builds up is His work. Jesus says He and He alone builds up the church. Our job is to seek the kingdom first (not ours) and His righteousness.

To do this we need to get to know Him and the power of His resurrection. Really that means overcoming by His power and not our own. My pastor said to me one day that God was giving him a church building and he was excited about it, this became clearer later on. The lady whose people we had met with before had asked him to come in with them and form one church in the new building she and her people had built. Oh the joy, God's people meeting together in unity and harmony to worship the Lord. Well so we thought, guess what? I was having trouble accepting this lady; she was a woman and a ministering leader in God's church. In those days this type of thing wasn't really accepted, possibly even today in some circles. God spoke to my heart and said she was His anointed and I got a realisation and wonderful peace and having put this thing is His hands which hasn't ever left me about woman ministers to this day, (though I question some as leaders). Once I got the peace from God I really started to enjoy this ladies ministry, she had a wonderful singing voice and used it in praise and worship to a great advantage. I loved it. I remember one communion service which she was taking, she led the people, in praise and worship and was exalting the Lord, and the presence of God was unbelievable. She gave an altar call and seven people got saved. Her call was evangelising there was no doubt about it. I heard her trying to teach one time and it was awful; each to their own that's why the body of Christ is made up of many parts.

Things seemed to be going along okay for a while. I got to know many of her people and we got on well, preaching, teaching, evangelism, prayer and worship were the order of the day, a great balance. There was no outward sign that there was anything amiss. I had just sat down with my wife and kids to attend a morning service and I felt the Lord speak to my spirit that the pastor and board were putting the lady minister out of the church; it hit me like a bolt of lightning. I remember saying under my breath no, no, not again. After the service I didn't say anything to anybody but during the week I went around to her house to see if it was the Lord speaking to me. She confirmed what I felt and again I felt like a child that was losing one of its parents to a divorce. Again there was a wonderful mix of ministry that was feeding the flock the church was growing and the people were settled. When the news hit the church this time it was big. I said to the pastor that I had come with, later on down the track, "If you ministers were not getting on too well why you didn't let the people know about it so that something could be worked out. If that didn't happen, I personally would have prepared to leave her and her people with the building that she had built and rented a hall or something to worship in". He didn't agree. Now to be fair, the minister and board may have had a reason to do what they did and felt it was the right thing to do, but I'm blowed if I could see it so I left and went with her as she was starting another church in a school hall. In those days it had been really hard for her to minister in much of Australia as she was a woman. This lady, who had a wonderful evangelistic calling had been invited to South Africa at times to minister and they loved her. She drew huge crowds and was asked to stay but Australia was her home. I don't believe that she really overcame what happened to her when she lost her building and was asked to leave the church by the so called eldership. I believe it broke her heart. The new church, which others and myself helped start with her lasted a few years and grew quite fast but in myself I sensed that all was not well. What had happened in the past, manifested in her preaching and worship and the church eventually closed. This again caused a lot of upset with the people. Being a father myself, I came to realise through the word of God and just life experiences that I or we, my wife and I, had a responsibility to bring up our kids where they could trust us and come to us in time of need. Through these situations of the churches splitting, people stopped going, and many for some time. I read once that when a thing like this happens, people can only take so much of this and after two or three times will stop going to church because who could they trust in the leadership. There has been a tendency over the years that when people leave a fellowship to say it's their fault, never the fault of leadership. I believe the way we set up leadership or the way leadership sometimes comes about can be so wrong, I will get into that a bit later.

We live in a world that have leaders that debase truth and lie through their teeth to get into power, then treat it as nothing they did was wrong! They beat their chests letting us know how wonderful they are to come to the place of such authority. This may happen in the world, but not in the church. I believe that many so called church leaders do not know or understand their responsibility as leaders. I believe that they have been set up far too early and don't know God well enough for the role they have been put in, possibly by others or even themselves. God is not looking for dictators but people who have a true father's heart. People that can move mountains by faith but don't have the love of the father don't mean a hill of beans to God. Jesus said in Matthew 23:11 (NIV) the greatest among you will be your servant, verse 12 for whoever exalts himself will be humbled and whoever humbles himself will be exalted. Mark 9:33 (NIV) They came to Capernaum. When he was in the house he asked them, "What were you arguing about on the road?" but they kept quiet because on the way they had argued about who was the greatest. Verse 33 (NIV) sitting down, Jesus called the twelve (who had been called to be leaders of the church) and said "If anyone wants to be first, he must be very last, and the servant of all". What Jesus is saying, if you are called on would you like to be a true leader in the church, His church, then you need to humble yourself to serve the flock and not the other way around. I think that many leaders think they can almost do what they like and get away with it. As a natural father I came to realise we had a responsibility to serve our children, to keep them clothed, housed and educated. It's not as though we didn't make mistakes; we did, but they knew that we loved them and they could come to us when the chips were down and we were there for them (I think).

My wife has been with the Lord for some years now and my relationship with my kids is possibly stronger than ever. I am so glad that it started when they were little snots, when they were small enough that I could give them a good hiding because I can't do that now; they do it to me. They still come to me for advice and money, mostly money, only kidding. I told them if they didn't behave I would spend their inheritance; they don't know it but I almost have. What I'm saying is true leadership is about laying your life down for others, just like Jesus did. He died that we could have life, and not just life, but live more abundantly (above the common life). John 10:10 (RSV) Jesus said that He would build his church and us humans to keep our grubby little hands off it. Our job is to seek His kingdom and His righteousness.

# 10

# Huff and Puff of Man's Endeavours

Since I have been born again much of the building of the church has been by the huff and puff of man's endeavours, not by the truth and spirit of God. When I look back over the short years I have been part of the church (40 odd) and seen many so called leaders come and go. Fallen by the wayside, TV personalities, men that have come to minister to us in a congregational situation, men that have come to town to bring the word of God and then not long after fallen away because of some sin of lust or pride, trying to build the church of God their way and not the way of the Lord. When I have seen the harm and devastation it has done to the babies, younger Christians and Christians generally, I have too often wondered why more advanced men and women of faith haven't done something to stop it. I see a very deceiving undermining of the church of Jesus Christ going on today, and yet many seem to think its all ok; yet, Jesus, Paul, John, Peter, Jude and the others warn about it. The bible states the church of God is built on the foundation of the apostles and prophets with Christ Jesus himself as the chief cornerstone, Ephesians 2:20.(NIV) The apostle Paul is the one that we most are enlightened about in the

New Testament, besides Jesus, that is. The book of Acts speaks so much about his exploits and he wrote most of the letters to the churches. He understood about the way Jesus is intending to build the church. He was in tune with what the Holy Spirit was saying to him. He was a man lead by the spirit of God, which is quite remarkable when you think of his background. Paul hated the church and tried to destroy it at the beginning of its growth. He was a Pharisee (the self righteous religious nutters of the day, living by the strictest sect of his religion) Acts 26:4&5.(NIV) One of the reasons the church is missing the mark in many ways in the West is that there is a cost to do things Jesus Christ way. It means death to self and we must hear what the Spirit is saying to the Church. I believe that much of the church is a Martha type operation Luke 10:40&41 (NIV) encumbered about with much serving; possibly in some cases allowing pride and arrogance to come in thinking they are doing so much for God whilst others are not. Thinking they are building the kingdom of God without really hearing what the Spirit is saying. They presume that this is the right way of doing things. This is what Jesus wants without really asking him first.

When King David wanted to bring the Ark of God's presence back to its rightful place the first time, he missed the mark and it cost a man his life. God was rocking the cart and man tried to stop God from doing it. I believe God is starting to rock the cart that the church has tried to use to bring in His presence. The cart to me means the way of the world, we are told not to get caught up in the system of the world. Much of the church has been built by King Saul's type of ministry, taking the best for self controlling, legalistic, building monuments to self etc, always wanting to be out in front, huff, puff and bulldust. What I mean by the system of the world is, one way is to put in place or stepping up into authority people that shouldn't be in it. Some years ago I had a client that was the maintenance man of a high school. I went to see him one day to see if he needed any products that he was using of mine. He was really downcast and upset about something. I said "What's wrong, you okay?" He told me what had happened the day before! In the morning he had gone mad, as fathers often do, at his daughter about the state of her room. She turned around and gave him a mouthful of lip. This really upset him. He told her not to speak to her father like that and next time he would give her a clip behind the ear. The daughter must have told her teacher who reported it to a government department. Next thing he knew, two young officials from that office came around to see him to put him straight about "child abuse". Well, he said he put them straight about how they did not have a clue about life, having kids, or much at all if it came to that. He asked them both if they were married and one said yes but did not have children. He said they were young and had a know-it-all, along with a self-righteous attitude, (sounds like so many of the younger, so called, leaders in some of the churches today) all politically correct and controlling, the way things are heading in our society today. These young people, had possibly gone to a university, got a degree, and joined a government department, became some sort of youth advisor/worker or something and because they were given a title, they thought they knew it all, with far, far too much authority. Very dangerous (don't get me started). Sounds like the Nazi youth of Nazi Germany before the Second World War, when the youth of the land tried to get rid of anything with proper authority in the name of political cleansing. We in our society don't have such violent or outward display of ruthlessness that happened with that group. It's far more subtle than that, its control through fear by political correctness or not really understanding God and His word! The Governments of the land at the time, allowed, encouraged and put into place the young people to use them for betterment of the government's cause, to get rid of any perceived opposition and bringing fear on the population. Well the maintenance man at the end won out and nothing happen about the situation. To go through that type of thing, it's not very nice for anybody to endure. I know abuse goes on in our society but it must be handled correctly. Kids will lie about situations that could cause heartache for the parents (family). I have seen it happen and it can be very stressful and upsetting for those involved. To put young people through university, college or some institution to try and teach them how to handle family situations is ridiculous. Bringing up a family is far more complicated than learning a few rules at some campus, getting a degree and trying to put it into practice. It's living the experience and if you start to get your kids to show respect and love for you and others, you are a winner. It takes dedication, wisdom and hard work with a lot of prayers and mistakes. Paul used this situation of family to underline oversights of elders in the church. (We will go into that later).

As we go on in our Christian walk, things will not always go according to the way we would like them to go. Jesus never said that situations would always be easy; in fact he said that we would endure trials. When we gave our lives to God through Jesus Christ we are justified through faith and have peace with God through Jesus Christ but it means that we also have to come to a place of trust and learn that our lives are not our own but His. Jesus said he would build the church and the church is us, people, not buildings, as it has been wrongly said over the years. So there is a process of elimination going on, elimination of us that He might be manifest through us, that the character of Christ might be seen in us. That means death to self, our strengths, self-will, ambitions etc that we come to a place of trusting him and not ourselves lest we boast about it. In Acts 14:21&22 (NIV) "They preached the good news in that city (Derbe) and won a large number of disciples. Then they returned to Lystra, Iconium and Antioch strengthening the disciples and encouraging them to remain true to the faith". We must go through many hardships to enter the Kingdom of God. I personally believe that is growing up in Him. Jesus said the kingdom of God is within. The Lord's Prayer "Our father which art in heaven, hallowed be thy name, thy kingdom come, thy will be done on earth as it is in heaven." The kingdom of God will be done as we learn and put into practise the things of God. This is done as we are led by the Holy Spirit, putting aside the things of the flesh, through good times and hard times, learning to put our hope in Him and not ourselves.

Man always wants to be first and yet much of what we do will come last in the kingdom of God. We have to come more to a place of doing things His way. We must learn to be guided by Him. It comes back to the heart thing again or the spirit of man.

Proverbs 16:2 (RSV) "All the ways of man are pure in his own eyes but the Lord weighs the spirit" (motives, heart). As we go on in God, it means to "grow up" which I do not see much in the church of God in the West today, in some sense, it has gone backwards! Being deceived can be a very subtle thing. Much of the church in the West, I believe is run more like a capitalist type operation, money has become the all consuming God, and what we can get out of it. The cross in many cases has been tossed out the window! We must rethink where we are going and start to grow up in God! To grow up means "allowing time" for this to happen and as a father watching your children "grow up" there is a process of change that goes on. As a parent you see this and hopefully you can move in your thinking to keep in reality with it. As the children grow, it's up to the parents to help, encourage, correct and at times, chastise where necessary. I guess we all want the best for our kids. It must be in love and patience, not trying to force your will on them, allowing them to grow up with balance and a will to love and respect you regardless of the mistakes you make.

# 11

# Give us a King like other nations

We live in a world that wants everything now, instant this, instant that got to have it now. When you see a kid in a shopping centre playing up because they can't get their own way for something, they make you feel like moving away from them hoping their mother will shut them up. As we all grow in God we all have to be patient, learning to be content with what God has given us. Unless we do that, God can and will allow us to go through some experience that will help us grow and that may not be nice. As we look back into the Old Testament to the book of I Samuel 8:1-4 (NIV) when Samuel grew old he appointed his sons as judges for Israel, verse 2, the name of his first born was Joel and the name of his second son was Abijah and they served at Beersheba, verse 3, but his sons did not walk in his ways. They turned aside after dishonest gain and accepted bribes and perverted justice, verse 4, so all the elders of Israel gathered together and came to Samuel at Ramah, verse 5, they said to him "You are old and your sons do not walk in you ways, now appoint a king to lead us such as all the other nations have". I believe that we, the church, are in a day of restoration, God is restoring back that which we have lost (truth) right back since the time of the very early church (Christian).

See, the church in the days of Samuel could see that things were not going to plan. In the days before King Saul, Israel had lost the Ark of the Lord to the Philistines but the Philistines could not handle it and in 1 Samuel 5 (NIV) (read it yourself) decided to send it back to the church (Israel). Chapter 6 as the Ark of the Lord was coming back to Israel, the people rejoiced, verse 13, but they too couldn't handle such a great event, verse 19, and it cost some their lives as they were bringing it back the wrong way! God is bringing his presence back into the church today and there is a right way and a wrong way of doing it. We must take time out to get into his presence and hear what the spirit is saying to the church. We need to get into his word and not presume that everything we are doing is ok. We must keep a humble heart before him as much as we can and like Mary sit at his feet and take in what he is saying. We won't necessarily understand what he is trying to get to us at the time but as we are willing it will sink in over time. It is not always easy because God has to build in us a maturity that can handle his presence, a people that know him and not just know about him. Jesus is building it over time.

As I said we live in a now generation, got to have it now, and I believe the church is caught up in that thinking. We might seem to be doing the right things, but are we? Have we really got on our knees and asked God if what we are doing is his will or our will? Are we rushing ahead full tilt, trying to build his church, what is really the motive of out heart. We need to ask God. There are things that are going on in the church that are not good and not of God, not His way of doing things. Before God sent Israel into the Promised Land he said to them in Exodus 23:27-30 (NIV), verse 27, "I will send my terror ahead of you and throw into confusion every nation you encounter. I will make all your enemies turn their backs and run", verse 28, "I will send the hornets ahead of you to drive the Hivites, Canaanites and Hittites out of your way", verse 29, "But I will not drive them out in a single year, because the land would become desolate and the wild animals too numerous for you", verse 30, "Little by little I will drive them out before you, until you have increased enough to take possession of the land". God is building His church little by little in us. Remember the kingdom of God is within. He is getting out much of the rubbish in our hearts so Christ can take his place as king there and be manifest through us. This is not salvation; this is growing up to bring forth the church that Jesus is coming for. It's a process of "little by little" because we couldn't handle it otherwise. God is building His church, His way, not our way. God is looking for true worshipers, in spirit and in truth.

Over the years seeing so many mess ups, you have to stop and take time to rethink, is this the church that Jesus is building or the church much of what man is building? The bible says "the letter kills but the Spirit gives life" We the church, quite often hear God telling us to go take the land, then we try to rush ahead and do it overnight. No wonder there is a lot of people falling away. Instead of bringing up new Christians as you would a child in your own family, we try to bring them on far too quickly, not little by little. Scripture teaches us that God didn't rush ahead after Adam and Eve sinned, before he bought Jesus into the world it took approximately five thousand years. A long time, but not for God, to us maybe! All the scripture written before Jesus was born were there by grace and the Holy Spirit, to teach us God's way of doing things. It is there to teach us, to help us understand that even though situations seem hopeless, God is still in charge. We live in a world that doesn't give us much hope and as Christians we are not to look at the hope in the world because it will disappoint us. Our hope is in Christ and in his ways. Paul wrote to the Roman Church that had a mixture of pagans and Jews. A people that had put their hope in what they had come out of, he was teaching them their hope was in the living God, in Christ Jesus, even though they would go through some very hard trials Romans 5:1-5, verse 1 (NIV). Therefore, since we have been justified (made right) through faith we have peace with God through our Lord Jesus Christ, verse 2, Through whom we have gained access, by faith into this grace in which we now stand. We rejoice in the hope of the glory of God, verse 3, Not only so, but we also rejoice in our sufferings (a hard thing to do) because we know that suffering produces perseverance (stick-ability), character (of Christ) and hope (trust in God) regardless of situations, verse 4, And hope does not disappoint us because God has poured out His love into our hearts by the Holy Spirit whom He has given us. I believe that the church is looking to bring back the glory of God. I believe that true born again Christians really want this. But just as David did, he messed up by trying to bring it in the world's way (cart). Just like David we need to seek the Lord on our knees, through scripture and the leading of the Holy Spirit to get back to the right way of doing things. We need to understand what the spirit is saying to the church over the years. We have allowed situations to arise that are harmful not only to the church but also to the person that the working of the ministry has been manifest out of. It's called eldership or leadership in the church. Proverbs 19:2 (NIV) "It is not good to have zeal without knowledge (wisdom, understanding) nor to be hasty and miss the way. We in the church of Jesus Christ are doing this big time with the way we are setting up young people and immature Christians into ministry. It has crept in slowly over a period of time undermining the work of the Lord. It seems so right but it is not. We need men and women of understanding to pray in the right way. Overtime I have noticed this coming into the church more and more, immature young people coming into a place of leadership that they could not handle, "zealousness without wisdom or knowledge of God and his ways". I have seen many young people fail because the oversight didn't know how to bring them through in humility and maturity. I believe much of the oversight was without much knowledge of how the church should function anyway. We the church, in many areas, have tried to rush ahead without growing up first! It's the "now" generation coming to light. Not just young people that it has been done to, but immature older people that are young in the Lord. We need to step back and take stock of where we are.

Just before David became king, the tribes of Israel came to show an undivided loyalty to him. 1 Chronicles 12:23-40 (NIV), these were people that could use all types of weapons. Just like the church today is made up of different types of ministries to do different operations in the church. There was a tribe which was different to the others, which is so essential to the way the church grows, a people of understanding 1 Chronicles 12:32 (NIV) "Men of Issachar", who understood the times and knew what Israel should do "These were the watchmen!" If there is such a need of people of understanding, watchmen, it would be now. We live in a generation of inside the church and outside the church, where things have crept in to undermine the very fabric of our society and church. Much of it, to the carnal mind seems ok, but it is not. Paul writing to the Roman church in Romans 1:18-32 (NIV) said this type of thing would be so and would only bring death to people that put these things into practice.

I was listening to the President of the USA speaking just after he was re-elected to that office, he said something like this "that it didn't matter what colour you were or country you came from, rich or poor, part of society you came from, gay (homosexual) or straight". Now what was he saying here, that gays were a normal, acceptable part of society. That the way they live and act was a normal way of living for some people. Yet the word of God completely condemns it as a wicked sin and perversion. Romans 1:26 to 32 (NIV). Is this what the President of the USA was saying? This is the way it came across to me. I heard that in the USA they are looking at their countries constitution to see what type of couples should be allow to wed and if they interpret it that homosexuals can, they will make it law right through the whole country. In New Zealand they have passed this law and a friend of mine who was a marriage celebrant lost her licence because she wouldn't marry homosexual couples. This is the thin edge of the wedge that will open up a Pandora's Box of worms!

BREAKING NEWS: To write a book takes time and since I have been writing this it has come to notice that the US Supreme Court has ruled in favour of same sex marriage on or about June 26th 2015! The ruling will affect all US states! Ireland a few weeks back voted in the same type of thing, God help us. How far have we fallen? You know, this shouldn't be a surprise to us, we in our so called Christian nations have not felt it worthwhile to retain the knowledge of God so he's giving us over to depraved minds. Even so called Christians, or Christians whose minds are still very carnal, seem to think that being gay is ok and they should be allowed to marry. God didn't make us to be homosexuals, our perverted lust did, driven on by Satan himself and because of depraved minds people are accepting this type of things more and more as normal. We in the church need to get back to some of the fundamentals of the way the church should operate, now I don't expect this to happen overnight!

As I said before that the way in which we are promoting young people and Christians to places of leadership is stupid and very wrong. In many cases all we are doing is feeding their egos and not building their character. Like a kid growing up that hates the word "NO". It means that they can't have it all their way all of the time. Sometimes the things they want are quite ok, but because they are not mature enough at the time we have to say "NO". Now this type of thing can put their little noses out of joint but it's good for them because they have to grow up and it helps them come to a place of maturity. If we spoil our kids, we do them and society a disservice but with God's help we win through. Promoting young people or young Christians too soon is not the way to go. Young people can be very zealous for God. I know I was as a young person. Exchange, help, guide but not promote young Christians over older people (mature Christians) 1 Peter 5:1-4 (NIV). To the elders among you, I appeal as a fellow elder, a witness of Christ's sufferings and one who will share in the glory to be revealed. Be shepherds of God's flock that is under your care, serving as overseers-not because you must, but because you are willing, as God wants you to be. Not greedy for money, but eager to serve, not lauding it over those entrusted to you, but being examples to the flock, and when the chief shepherd appears, you will receive the crown of glory that will never fade away! (The churches were going through some hard times and they needed mature shepherds to help them come through it!) Peter goes on to bring wisdom and correction to the young men right away after he wrote to the leaders or elders of the churches, hoping the younger men would see their place in the church. 1 Peter 5:5 "Young men, in the same way be submissive to those that are older". What way? Willingly, I believe he was saying, doing it with humility. The apostle then adds that humility is to be practise by every one! "All of you clothe yourselves with humility towards one another, because God opposes the proud but gives grace to the humble."

Now let's look at the life of Jesus Christ, the way he went up through the ranks until he was ready for ministry. It wasn't very exciting, a lot of responsibility and nobody could see his promotion coming. They thought he was only a carpenter, not a trade that God would bring you to a place of knowing God. Hey, I don't think he even went to Bible College. Jesus being a Jew would have had the Old Testament taught to Him, but really it was up to Him to get to know his God and He also had good parents. When we look at Jesus and His life before He came into His ministry, there are some points we need to look at and take stock of before we rush off and promote young people into the place of authority. Jesus grew up in a Jewish home. He would have been taught the Old Testament and the Law of Moses but because of all the things that had taken place as a baby and just after, His folks would have known that this lad had a calling on His life, that God had His hand on Him for some purpose.

We go to when Jesus was twelve years of age in Luke 2:41-52 (NIV). Every year His parents went to Jerusalem for the Feast of the Passover, verse 42, when He was twelve years old, they went up to the feast, according to the custom, verse 43, after the feast was over, while His parents were returning home, the boy Jesus stayed behind in Jerusalem, but they were unaware of it, verse 44, thinking He was in their company, (should have known better), they travelled on for a day. Then they began looking for Him among their relatives and friends, verse 45, when they did not find him, they went back to Jerusalem to look for Him, verse 46, after three days they found Him in the temple courts, sitting among the teachers, listening to them and asking them questions, verse 47, everyone who heard him was amazed at His understanding and His answers, verse 48, when His parents saw Him, they were astonished. His mother said to Him "son, why have you treated us like this? Your father and I have been anxiously searching for you?" verse 49, "Why were you searching for me?" He asked. "Don't you know I had to be in my father's house?" verse 50, but they did not understand what He was saying to them (Jesus was different to other boys, His folks should have known this is what God had put them through when He was a child and should have been aware of the situation a little more than they did), verse 51, then He went down to Nazareth with them and was obedient to them. But His mother treasured all these things in her heart, verse 52, and Jesus grew in wisdom and stature (maturity) and in favour with God and man. There He awaits God's timing (so important) to begin the ministry that God had called Him into. This took about another 18 years. Jesus didn't just rush into this ministry but grew in wisdom and stature or should we say "more" as He was already doing this, and in favour with God and man. How did He do this? We know that Jesus was a carpenter and without too much fear of contradictions learnt the trade from His earthly father who was also a chippy (carpenter). A carpenter those days could have been a stone mason as well. Somewhere after the temple situation and when He went home, He learnt His trade; let's say He was 15 years of age. The next time we hear of Jesus was with His mother at a wedding in Canna, John 2:1 (NIV). His father is not mentioned at all after the parents found Jesus in the temple when He was 12 years old, except to say He was a carpenter! I believe that Jesus' father had died! Jesus, being the eldest in the family, took over the family business and was the head of the family. We know Jesus had brothers and sisters Matthew 13:55&56, so this could have been hard work for Him. As a father myself, it is not always easy to bring up kids the right way. The little darlings will try you to the bone. It must have been hard for Jesus to do this. Siblings don't like taking orders from the other siblings and I guess Jesus didn't have it all His own way. I think we need to look at this situation as it was or could have been. We have to remember that at first His siblings didn't believe in Him as the Lord of Lord, King of Kings, and the Saviour of the world. They would have seen Him as the town folk did, as Jesus the man. Losing his earthly father would have had an impact on the family and this in itself could have caused the brothers and sisters to rebel to some degree against the authority Jesus had inherited.

Losing my own spouse made me see the impact it had on my own children, and it can be very devastating at times. I know I spend a lot of time before God for my children and me, and I thank God He's far bigger than the situation. Rosemary is with Jesus in glory now, in a far better place than we are in. I know losing someone close can have a big impact on you. To me it was 2008, just when the recession hit. Many businesses folded and I myself being self employed didn't have the will to push myself through the tough time as I had done in the past. Losing Rosemary I couldn't see the point to it. I felt the Lord leading me to look at the book of Job. Job lost everything, except his wife and his faith in God. He didn't really fully understand it, but he came to a place of trust which he never had before, he came to a greater relationship with his God, a greater revelation of who God is and this took Him on to a new insight of the greatness of God the father. God wants to manifest His glory through the church in a way that we as yet cannot possibly see, but I believe it will come one day. Jesus said He would build the church but has to kill us on the way. No flesh will inherit the kingdom of

God only that which is done in God, not necessary for God, will triumph in Glory.

You know "life is like a vapour". Compared to eternity it's not even a drop in the bucket, but this is the time God has given us to do His will His way. Let's seek God that we might do His will His way and not our own. Jesus is building His church; let us hear what He has to say. "Time Out" we need to listen to hear His voice. The way we do that is to get into His word, the bible, read it, meditate on it, and if we find it hard to understand, ask God to reveal it to us. 2 Timothy 2:15 (KJV) "Study to show thyself approved unto God a workman that needeth not to be ashamed, rightly dividing the word of truth". We need to pray and seek His face. Sometimes we need to be like an old cow which regurgitates its cud and chews on it over and over again, getting all the goodness out of it. The bible says to "pray continually" 1 Thessalonians 5:17. What it means is our reliance is on God and not ourselves (that's why I love to speak in tongues). Jesus understands what we go through because He himself as a human being went through life's hard times as well. The Bible says that Jesus grew in favour with God and man. For this to happen He would have had to be in contact with people. He would have had his friends and relations but also in His trade He would have mixed with people of the world. You can imagine, let's say, that two Jewish businessmen were discussing about some townhouses they were about to get built. Mat said to Saul "Which quote do you think we should go for?" Saul replied "Jesus' I reckon, He's a bit dearer than the rest but boy you get a great job and there is no hassle afterwards with the finished work". See Jesus came to a better place of maturity through good times and bad before He came into His ministry. He knew what we go though because He Himself went through it. This is in step with what Paul told Timothy to do in setting up elders (overseer for the church) in 1 Timothy 3:4-7 (NIV) "He must manage his own family well and see that his children obey him with proper respect, verse 5, If anyone does not know how to manage his own family, how can he take care of God's church?" Jesus, I believe did this when He took over the care of the family after Joseph died. Even though He wasn't married, he still, I believe knew in human terms, how to look after children or young people and His mother, verse 7, He must also have a good reputation with outsiders, so that He will not fall into disgrace and into the devils trap. As we have said before "Jesus found favour with God and man".

Jesus came into His ministry at the age of about 30 years old, which in Jewish tradition was the age that people went into the priesthood. Up to this time He wasn't seen by anybody to have God's hand on him, except perhaps by His mother. Over the years I have seen many young people and young Christians put into places of authority that they shouldn't be in; especially in places of oversights in the church. To me this is sillier than a bag full of cut snakes. If we were to take Paul's insight of oversights or elders (shepherds, pastors etc) in the church today, a big percentage wouldn't be doing the job. Many leaders don't have children old enough to be in submission, with respect to these leaders. I believe this would have to be when the kids reach an age they almost willingly pay respect. Maybe 10-12 years of age. Sometimes it could be done reluctantly, showing respect that is. Children can be little darlings (not) at times. The church today can be and in many cases set up for younger people. They lead the music and worship which is ok because it is not too much authority in running the church. When you hear young people starting to call themselves "pastor" and this in a lot of cases has been brought on by the oversight above them. Many of the oversights today, under Paul's leadership wouldn't be in the place they are at because he would not have classed them as mature enough to handle the church in God's way. We in the church, look forward to leaders on personalities, looks, abilities to speak well, sing, pray, gifts of the Spirit, etc. All these and more do not necessarily make you a leader in the church. They can if not handled right, build your ego and not your character. Let's look at Paul for a moment and why he was one of the great apostles.

# 12

# School of hard knocks

Acts 9:15&16 (NIV) "But the Lord said to Ananias, Go! This man (Saul or Paul) is my chosen Instrument to carry my name before the Gentiles and then kings and before the people of Israel. I will show him how much he must suffer for my name". There was a process of hard knocks in Paul's life that bought him to the place of maturity. It's through the school of hard knocks that we all learn of God and get to know him. As the scriptures say "it's not good to be zealous without knowledge, wisdom and understanding of ourselves and God, then rush ahead and miss the mark, Proverbs 19:2 (NIV). Young people can be very zealous for God and want to rush ahead but in most cases don't have a clue and as I said before a lot of their oversight don't either. We in the church think that all is ok but believe me, it is not. We need to stop and like Mary sit at Jesus feet to get the church back into the right order of things. When we look back into the word of God, we see that those that did and achieved much for God went through the school of hard knocks. Many were anointed long before they came to a place God had told he would bring them to. David was anointed to be king but that didn't come into place for about another 14 years. Anybody that knows about David's life during that time would know that he went through some real hard times. He even came to a place that even though God had anointed him to rule over Israel he said that surely Saul would kill him. Moses was a man that God had chosen to lead his people out of bondage. Moses tried this first by his own strength. He killed an Egyptian thinking that his people would understand that God was with him but they didn't. Exodus 2:14, the man said, who made you ruler and judge over us? Are you thinking of killing me as you killed the Egyptian? Then Moses was afraid and thought "what I did must have become known", verse 15, when Pharaoh heard of this he tried to kill Moses, but Moses fled from Pharaoh and went to live in Midian. Moses did become ruler and judge over the Israelites but 40 years later, after he came to a place where he thought he was a nobody it was then that God started to use him. All the skills he had learnt growing up in Pharaohs house (the way of the world) came to nothing. God had to retrain him in his ways; he had to get Egypt out of Moses. When Moses was sent back to speak to Pharaoh and told him to let God's people go, he was ready! Up till then he was looking after his father-in-laws sheep, and he became one of the world's most humble men! He got to know God and learnt to trust in him and not of himself as he had done when he killed the Egyptian. When he faced Pharaoh, he came across opposition and Pharaoh said NO even when the Lord brought calamities on him and his nation. Pharaoh said he would kill Moses. Even the Jews, who he was trying to save out of bondage, turned against him, but God had built a trust and resolve in Moses that he stood his ground till he got the job done. Moses had learnt to know God through the mundane things, so God used him in the bigger things! Abraham was told by God he would be the father of many nations Genesis 17:4 (NIV). Up to that time Abram (that was his name before God changed it) had produced a son who was named Ishmael but he wasn't the son of promise, but before this came about Genesis 12:1-3 (NIV). The Lord had said to Abram "leave your country, your people and your father's household and go to the land I will show you, verse 2, I will make you into a great nation and I will bless you. I will make your name great and you will be a blessing, verse 3, I will bless those who bless you, and whoever curses you I will curse and all the people on earth will be blessed through you".

In Genesis 12:1-3 (NIV) Abram was told by God he would be the father of a great nation. Up until this time Abram had no children and he was 75 years of age. He wasn't a young man but God said he would produce a child through him, the child of promise. Like all of us when things don't go to our own plans we start to presume on the way things should go. Because he did not have an heir, the one God had promised, for the first 25 years after he left his home, Abram started to get a little anxious about this promise coming to pass. First he said his servant would be his heir but God said no, Genesis 15:4 (NIV). Then the word of the Lord came to him "this man will not be your heir but a son coming from your body will be your heir". Sarai, Abram's wife was also getting anxious about not having children. Those days not having children was classed as a reproach. Children were classed as wealth, so you could have been looked down on. Abraham and Sarah (God changed their names) did finally have a son that God was looking for! It was when their use by date was finished; it was when their ability to produce in the natural was gone! It was then that God must have said to himself "Right, now I can use them and they begat (I love that word) the son of promise, Isaac". Being married for 37years, I can understand about how women feel about not having children. My wife and I were married for 13 years before we had our first child. Rosemary took it quite hard seeing her friends having babies and we couldn't produce. I know my heart went out to her. I got checked up and she got checked up. They said I had problems because of a low sperm count. Rosemary was told that she had a low percentage rate of producing herself and it wasn't such a good idea because her kidneys were weak, so we started the process of adopting a child. This in itself took 5 years to come about, so it was a long wait. I know as her husband, I spent a lot of time praying for her because I felt for her. I felt her pain and time was marching on. One night we came home from church, the kids had done some skit or something. As we got through the door Rosemary broke down. I realised what it was about seeing those kids up on stage had reminded her of not having her own and not knowing when we would. Again my heart went out to her. The next morning the phone rang and it was the adoption agency saying they had a little girl for us, come in a couple of days and pick her up. Not having anything prepared because we didn't know what sex we were getting, panic set in! After Rosemary calmed me down we got things sorted and I remember going to pick Tanya up, which was very exciting. Rosemary and I were walking up a set of stairs to go to the offices of the agency and in front of us was a person carrying a little girl dressed in a pink suit with a pink bonnet on her head. The child was draped over the person's shoulder and was looking down at us. In her mouth was a dummy; her big eyes were looking at us and we didn't know at the time that this was the child we would get. Rosemary said, "Oh, what a beautiful baby" It was like walking up the stairs with two people, she was beside herself. The baby was probably thinking, "If these are the dopes that will take me home, I hope they know what they are letting themselves in for", and we didn't. Oh the joys of kids. We named the kid Tanya, which means Russian Princess. Well, she was and still is my little princess; she bought so much joy into the house. I'm so proud of Tanya, I couldn't have wished for a better daughter. I'm proud of both our kids, but don't tell them. Well, after waiting thirteen years you can imagine what Rosemary was like, a clucky chook, but who could blame her. About three years later Rosemary fell pregnant with Stephen our son. Hey, they said we couldn't have kids and anyway Rosemary's kidneys were weak and she shouldn't anyway. Once she found out she was expecting a child, she got all excited again. There was no talk of an abortion, it wasn't even discussed. We just thanked God for it.

The kids were quite different to bring up. Tanya was easy; Stephen was hard so I reckon kids are sent to try us. As they got older the reverse happened. When Tanya was 7 years old, Rosemary's kidneys started to deteriorate. The doctors joined a fistula to a vein on Rosemary's left arm. This was so they could place needles into her arm. The needles were attached to tubes that fed her blood into a dialysis machine, which in turn cleaned the blood. She used to go to the hospital 3-4 times a week, so it really tied up our time, but hey, she was my wife and mother of the brats. I remember the first week after she had to go to get the dialysis done; we had to get up early at about 5am if I remember rightly, for about a week and take her to the hospital (which was quiet at that time). The kids used to get wheelchairs and race around the wards in them until they got told off by some matron. "I didn't know who the children belonged to! Mine wouldn't carry on like that!" After this activity was stopped the kids reckoned they should be allowed to have some sweets out of the sweet vending machine. Every morning we went into the hospital they would go and stand by it, hoping. These were real hard times as the kids had to get to school and preschool. I had a business to run to try and bring in some money as they reckoned it was my job to feed them as well. Some church friends of ours, Stuart and Karen Nelson, were great. Karen would pick the kids up from school and take them home to her place. I would call in after work to pick them up and she would have tea ready for me as well. Thank you Nelsons, you guys have been a real blessing, not only then but over the years. For some reason Karen couldn't pick up the kids after a while so we put them into day-care. Karen did this for a short while. Going to pick them up one evening I remember crying out to the Lord as the children needed to get from school to day care and I was all over the place with my work, it would have been almost impossible to do. A Christian lady heard about our plight and said she would drop the kids off at day-care. We at the time did not know her but Karen did and said it would be fine. Again I am so grateful to that lady and the Lord for supplying our needs at the time. Before Rosemary went on dialysis we could easily have lost her. Her health deteriorated so much, she lost a lot of weight, her eyes sunk back into her head and she was tired all the time. I would come home from work and she was quite often asleep on the sofa. The doctors warned us that if she got sick we must get her to hospital ASAP. I didn't fully understand this and Stephen our son got the flu or something. Rosemary developed similar symptoms. Thinking she only had the flu I said not to worry about it. Rosemary said no and rang the doctor just in case. He told her to get into hospital right away, so we did. What a dope I was! The hospital put her onto dialysis right away and she was in for a week. When she came home after that week we still had to take her into hospital every day for check ups for another week, I spoke about this before when the kids took off in wheelchairs. We were sitting down to a meal not long after she went on dialysis and I looked at her. I couldn't believe how her colour had come back and how well she looked, it was unbelievable.

Dialysis gave some sort of real life back to us and we were grateful that God had used this method to do it, but it can tie you down. Four times a week Rosemary had to go into Perth to get her blood cleansed which in itself is great but we really couldn't go on holidays or away for more than a couple of days. We loved our holidays with the kids and quite often other friends. Mind you after what the kids did at the hospital I could have easily left them home and taken the dog. I know I was so grateful to God for allowing Rosemary's health to come back, even though there were restrictions to our lives, we could function as a family. Getting a new kidney was almost impossible or even so you had to wait a long time, but I still cried out to God on behalf of my wife. One morning I had got up as I am not a late sleeper, Rosemary was still in bed and I noticed she was a little downcast. I asked her what was wrong; she said that she hated the thought of getting those big needles put into her arm that day. My heart went out to her and just pleaded with God. Well, like when we got Tanya, the hospital rang the next day and said "Come and get your new kidney" (not baby). The operation was a complete success and when Rosemary came home they had put her on steroids for awhile to bulk her up or something. She got a little porky which I had never seen her like that before. The kids and I gave her a hard time over it but when they took her off the steroids she went back to the old Rose, beautiful as ever. Even though Rosemary had to get a check up every three months and she was on anti-rejection medication, she never had any problems with the kidney. I am so grateful that she had 17 good years with me and the kids after the operation. Rosemary never died with kidney failure, but cancer took her. Rosemary always showed grace and love to others like I had never seen before. Not only was she a beautiful person but through her hard times which she had many (she was married to me and had two brats for kids) she helped me see God in a way that I have never seen him before. There was a birthday party at our house one year for me. We only had birthday parties for me as I like presents. My friend Rod was telling everybody what a great chap I was and Tanya wanted also to say something. Through her speech she bought her mother into the conversation and broke down, letting people know how much suffering and how many times Rosemary had gone into hospital, for one reason or another.

Rosemary came over and put her arm around her to console her, telling Tanya it was alright. This just confirmed what a great lady I had married.

King David said that when he got to heaven he would see the son he had lost. I am not sure if this will be possible for me because Rosemary will be so far up the ladder of rewards that I won't be able to reach her. After we lost Rosemary the Lord spoke to my heart and said we were not our own but we are bought with a price, we belong to him. Losing Rosemary has been extremely hard but I believe it has also helped me see and understand God in a new way. Just after Rosemary got the new kidney, the maintenance department supervisor of the dialysis machines of another hospital just happened to be a client of mine. I told Fred, the head of the department, that Rosemary had got a new kidney. He looked extremely surprised and said it must be a new record. I asked why and he explained that you don't get kidneys after 9 months on dialysis, praise God. On a lighter side of things, when they joined the fistula to the vein on Rosemary's left arm it rose up a bit and looked a bit knotty. At night I could hear the blood rushing through it when she had her arm on the pillow, also if you touched the vein you could feel the blood rushing through it. When they stuck the needles in afterward they left marks up her arm. One hot night we were at a wedding reception and I noticed a lady that was sitting opposite us looking at Rosemary's arm. I said to Rose later that she must have thought she had been shooting up. I should have told the lady that we snorted. We had a laugh over it!

# 13

# Which God?

The word 'hero' has been bandied around to such an extent these days we almost forget the real meaning of it and because the world needs someone to follow or worship they look for a person or personality that stands out. In today's society it doesn't seem to matter if that person, who along the way of achieving their goal or ambition has walked over others, wrecked their marriage and relationship with their children, got into practices that are dubious to say the least. It doesn't seem to matter what they do as long as they stand out and please the masses. Years ago hero meant to most people "a person noted or admired for mobility, courage and outstanding achievements", a person who in a sense, lays down or risked their life for others. But in today's world we would have added other achievements into the meaning. Sport is one that comes to mind quite readily. Society looks and treats many sports people like some sort of hero or god. While I personally admire a person that has worked hard at this chosen profession, I don't see them as heroes. Today if you are in the big league of your sport you can and in many cases, get a very good pay packet. It really behoves one to play well as you could lose all your benefits and job. Just before the Second World War the German people looked to Nazism and their leader Adolf Hitler to get them out of the mess their country was in. Other countries followed along the same line, eg Italy and Japan. When the smoke cleared and the cost was counted, approximately 60 million people had lost their lives. What a cost, not only to them but also the allies who had to stop their madness. The countries of Germany, Italy and Japan had put men up as hero's or even god's to look to and be guided by; all they got was defeat and destruction. The Bible says to love your enemies which the allies did by helping these countries rebuild. Why oh why has the church fallen into the same type of thing by promoting young people and young Christians to be called pastors and used in places of leadership that they really haven't a clue about. We also in many cases also look to TV preachers, who travel the world extracting money out of Christians that cannot see through these deceivers true desires  Are we looking for leadership that seems to stand head and shoulders above others, as King Saul was, and look how he lead the people of the day? The people were so deceived that they wanted a leader like the rest of the nations of the world and God gave them one! I used the graphic illustration of the Nazis etc to point out how we in the church can go off the rails and be deceived if we really don't seek and ask the Lord to point out true leadership and the right way to promote it. Peter is a good example of a person that was zealous for God but didn't always use wisdom or understanding of himself and God, but because he had a true love for Jesus, he turned out to be one of the great apostles. If we look into the word of God from Acts through the letters etc we find for any situation that required the mind of God in leadership, they used wisdom, prayer and fasting. Just as the world uses the word hero wrongly in many situations, so we in the church use the name pastor wrongly. We set up young people in places that they shouldn't be, we allow them to perform and build them up where their egos and not their character are being pumped up. We, the church have got it so wrong. It's time we all started to grow up.

I believe Jesus is building His church and some good things have been done along the way. I also believe that He is restoring things that we had at the beginning but were lost or pushed out of the way and He is revealing the truth of them back to the church. When Constantine the Roman General and Emperor, in about 300AD started to take control of the church, hey, you don't argue with Emperor Generals. Satan must have laughed all the way to the bank when the Emperor said he had a vision of the cross in the heavens and that gave licence to take over the church with his military and political powers, which has lasted for many years under that type of rule. I bet, if I was a betting man, Constantine didn't check out to see which God gave him the vision. Like so many people today that say they have visions, or go up to heaven or see angels etc. don't check it out first, as the word tells us to. They, I believe go along with this thing as it make them seem so spiritual to others as well as themselves. The church, the true church, the one lead by the Spirit of Christ and guided by the revealed word, after Constantine came on board the true church went out the window and the man made church started to seemingly take over. I believe that out of this the Catholic Church evolved, which is run by the will and flesh of man! Coming out of that church, which has millions of followers, I have come to realise and believe, without the fear of contradiction, very few are born-again by God's Holy Spirit, in other words saved. Being a Catholic, Baptist, Church of England, or any other church member doesn't save us, Jesus does. The first thing we must do is to turn away from sin, in other words, repent and make him Lord of our lives, there is no other way, it has nothing to do with what church we belong to! God has only one true church and is made up of true born-again believers, with Jesus Christ as head and Lord. God will not be mocked and always had people that he could use to bring back truth to build His church and the gates of hell shall not prevail against Gods' real church. God wants his church to go on to maturity so he is and will continually reveal his truth to us. Our job is to continually accept God's truth and give in to Him. Let us not be like many of Jesus disciples and turn back because they could not accept his hard teaching, John 6:60&66. (NIV)

    Let us be like Simon Peter who said Jesus had the words of eternal life, John 6:69 (NIV) so they could not turn back. Sometimes going on in God is hard and we have trouble accepting it. I found that when things got hard to accept in my marriage, the word of God would challenge me about loving my wife or not being harsh to her; yes we had our differences and sometimes it got to my flesh. Many times I would cry out to God to help me be a better husband and help me control my temper. I loved the Lord and wanted to serve him the best I could. Possibly loving my wife was the greatest achievement I could do and by loving her

I was serving Christ. The bible likens Christ's relationship to the church as a marriage "we shall know the truth and the truth will set us free". Truth is a wonderful thing if we allow it to work in us. The word of God never ceases to amaze me; it is such a living word, getting right into the inner heart of us to bring life and liberty. Where the Spirit of God is, there is liberty (freedom) so we must allow him to control our hearts (spirit) more and more, even though we are saved by grace and faith in Jesus, he never takes away our free will. To come to a place of allowing our will to become his will. We need to come to a place where like Paul we become a "love slave", given over to him because we want to, just like a marriage, two individuals become one. It's a mystery and only God can do it. For the church to come to a place of greater maturity we need to change and this will be very hard for some because we are used to doing things the "status quo". Change is not always easy but like the cloud that led the people out of Egypt; if it moves so do we or we get left exposed to the elements and get sunburnt. The cloud was Israel's covering that protected them and leads them but they had to stay under it. As the word of God brings us to a new revelation we must move with it. I believe God is moving, Jesus is building His church, let's stay the course!

As God has moved on over the years to bring back truth, justification through faith not by works, baptisms, the gifts of the Spirit etc, we must be awake to understand what is going on. Being in Christ is a growing process as individuals and as the church. Peter and Paul use the analogy of milk as one way of speaking to new Christians about having to grow up so they could feed on the meat of the word of God and go on to maturity 1 Corinthians 3:2 (NIV). "I give you milk, not solid food, for you were not yet ready for it, indeed, you are still not ready, therefore let us leave the elementary teaching about Christ and go on to maturity", Hebrews 6:1 (NIV). Its God's will that the church moves on and Paul, when he told Timothy and Titus to set up elders in the churches one thing he had in mind was that the elders were mature enough to have their own children be in subjection to them. Why, because they could rule their own household and thus be mature enough to in some part, rule the church. As a Christian of some years and having been in the church for some years and seen the mess ups, I have to question what is going on. Speaking to a friend of mine the other day, possibly more of an acquaintance who does not go to a Pentecostal church but one of the other denominations, I found this guy had a great love for the Lord and I enjoyed talking to him. The subject got onto bust ups in churches and the harm it does. I was telling him of my experiences when he told me he could not go through another bust up, it shattered him too much. He went on to say that the only ones that lead in the church should be those that don't want to lead; I think I understood what he meant. Young people or Christians generally do not have a clue, and if they do not go through the right process of leadership, can and do grow up to be controlling, dogmatic and in some cases go right off the rails. The people in church don't need this. We need leaders with a father's heart; we need to get back to a place of rightly dividing the word of God. Faith in itself is not enough. Faith without love doesn't mean much in God's eyes. Paul in 1 Corinthians

13:2&3 (NIV) puts it this way "if I have the gift of prophecy and can fathom all mysteries and all knowledge and if I have a faith that can move mountains but have not love I am nothing. If I give all I possess to the poor and surrender my body to the flames but I have not love I gain nothing." What love was Paul talking about? I believe it was the first love, the love we can easily let slip by doing, doing, doing! Losing that intimacy and with that we don't allow God to deal with our hearts. The first love to God is the most important one; everything else takes second place. We must get back to our first love, where he becomes Lord once more and not our own endeavours.

My father who was a builder back in Upper Hutt, New Zealand when I was a young lad didn't do things in a small way. He had a good size conduction company, a joinery shop, logging mill up in the hills and a pre fabricating site, he had about 70 to 80 folk working for him at times I heard. I remember going up to the logging mill with Dad one day and seeing this huge mountain of sawdust, well to me it looked like a mountain, being a small kid. Dad was a good provider for the family but I felt it hard to get too close to him up till after the time I came to Australia. That started to change as time went on and Dad slowed down in his work, I don't think he really stopped, well not until Mum got Alzheimer's disease then he tried his utmost to look after her. With the help of my elder brother Keith and his wife Pam they did a great job, thank you blokes from the bottom of my heart. This went on until they had to put Mum in a home! I think this nearly broke Dad's heart! Before this took place, Mum and Dad would come and visit our family in Perth and we would go back and see them and the rest of the mob in NZ. One day when we were visiting them in NZ, Dad took me aside and said "Don't ever put your business in front of your family." I feel to some degree that Dad knew that with all his working to build his enterprises the he neglected his family! It wasn't so much the material things! We never went without; it was that relationship of the heart that I believe he missed. Our visiting each other brought a closeness that we missed before. Dad went out of his way; to me it seemed, to make up for lost time. I remember one time, just before my family and I were about to head out to the airport to come back to Perth I told Dad that I loved him! He said that he also loved me. Well, that blew me away as Dad was from the old school, you know, kids should be seen and not heard type of thing! I think that was the first time he had said that to me, I was overjoyed.

# 14

# God's Commandments

Jesus said in John 14:15 (NIV) "If you love me, keep my commandments". Was He talking about the letter of the 10 commandments? No, it was His revealed word given to us by his leading, teaching, and correction etc of the word of God by the Holy Spirit. The bible is trying to show there is a new way, a better way of doing God's will, not by the letter of the law which kills but by the spirit of Christ that brings life. This is why God allows us to go through hard times, it should make us come to a place of realising that it is not our strength but in His that we stand. As we go though hard times it will and should help us to grow into maturity a little bit more with our walk with Him. Paul who was a real father to the churches, knew how important it was for oversights of his church to have like minded men and women that had bought up a family in the natural, who through good times and bad times had come to a place when the kids could make up their own minds and show respect to their parents. This showed Paul that these folk had put effort into the bringing up of their family. It was in a sense a benchmark on how things should be run in the church, by people with an understanding of life, not just head knowledge! Now I don't believe in the letter of the law on anything really but, when over the years of being in the Pentecostal or Charismatic church and have seen the mess ups we have had and in a lot of cases, missed the mark in allowing God to build His church. God is sitting back looking and thinking "well, it's about time correction is bought to the kids, they are messing up again." (I understand that not every married couple have children, but many come to a place of leadership because of some hard times they go through). Paul, who understood the father heart of God, wanted only people with a father's heart run the church. That famous scripture comes to mind in John 3:16 (NIV) "For God so loved the world that He gave His one and only son that whoever believes in Him shall not perish but have eternal life".

When you look back into the Old Testament, Israel seemed to sin more than they were, at least, trying to be righteous before God. The world itself was always sinning against God. We didn't deserve a saviour to come and die (to take the place for us) for our wickedness and rebellion. It was the father heart that so loved us that I believe He couldn't help Himself, He had to do it, we didn't deserve it but He did it anyway. Paul wanted true leaders as overseers of the church, people that had come to some kind of discipline, proving that they could rule with fairness and authority thus instilling into those that they were over, respect for them. Unfortunately, we in the church can have and do have "wolves in sheep's clothing", people that will come out from among us (Christians) to draw people to themselves to rule over them. Not with the true love of the father but because they want to be in charge, controlling with a dictatorial attitude. True fathers know how to let go, knowing how to love the sheep with all their mistakes they make along the way. Acts 20:17 (NIV) "From Miletus Paul sent to Ephesus for the elders of the church", verse 27 "For I have not hesitated to proclaim to you the whole will of God, keep watch over yourselves and all the flock of which the Holy Spirit has made you overseers, be shepherds of the church of God." Notice he called the elders (plural not single). I believe this could have been a safeguard for the church and not run by a one man band. When Paul set up the eldership in the church he chose mature men, people that had been through some sort of place of exercising authority to others i.e. their children and they in turn respected their parents because of it. They had run the family well, first the natural then the spiritual.

To say that I am against young people ministering would not be true. I know I was very zealous when I got saved, wanted to tell everybody about Jesus. Paul did the same sort of thing at the beginning of his ministry and nearly got killed until some of the oversight sent him back to his home town Tarsus. I have no doubt that there were other Christians there whom Paul had fellowship with; also I believe that Paul could have been in Tarsus about 13 years before God started to open up his ministry, being zealous is one thing, but now he had a little bit more wisdom and knowledge! Before the time that Paul was to be used there had been a move of God among the Greeks in Antioch, Acts 11:20-21 (NIV). The church sent Barnabas from Jerusalem to have a look see, Acts 11:22-25.(NIV) Barnabas must have felt Paul was ready, went to Tarsus, got Paul and bought him back to Antioch to help him teach the new disciples, Acts 11:23-26 (NIV). What I am trying to get across here was that Paul, the great apostle, had to take time out to learn his ministry, it just didn't happen overnight. I know as young people, keen as, we still had to learn and allow God to promote us. I believe that the way young people are promoted today in the church is stupid and wrong. They might be full of the Holy Spirit as Jesus was before His long fast but they still have to overcome by growing up into maturity. Matthew 4:1 Jesus was led by the Spirit into the desert to be tempted. God did this so He would overcome His temptations by denying himself things that he needed to get by with (food, shelter etc) and as well the devils temptations! When we see young people in charge of groups, they are, in a lot of cases, people that are confident (overly in many cases), bubbly (which young kids will draw to), quite often very good musicians, singers and leaders of worship, youth leaders doing the work of evangelists in schools etc and they really love what they are doing. Take that away from them and where do they stand with God. Talking to a young man who had done a job of lead guitar in church worship, he told me he did it because he wanted to be up there in front of the church. He's not doing that anymore, he seems to be going through some sort of wilderness experience at the moment, which I'm sure he will overcome. Leadership is more than running a show; it is about being obedient with a father and a mother's heart towards the will of God. This comes through the school of hard knocks. As I said before, set people up too early and all we do is increase their egos more than their character. God is not looking for superstars but humble hearts. We all have seen people crash and because we, as good old humans, have tried to build the church our way, Jesus said "I will build the church and the gates of hell will not prevail against it". So let's get back to a place of allowing Jesus to do it. The bible says that in the last days there will be a falling away in the church. I can understand this seeing the way we try to build the church, there is so much flesh involved. If we really want to see a true move of God we must allow him to lead us into maturity so we can handle it, in many cases I really don't think we are ready.

Years ago when I got saved and a few years after we seemed to have some great teachers coming through, people that had depth in what they said, people with years of experience. They would speak and we would listen with baited breath hoping they wouldn't stop. Over the years, we the church, thinking we know better started promoting younger people to speak. Now I am not saying they didn't have a calling on them and some of them I really admired their ministry, but not seeing the dangers that I see now, it started to teach me. Like a lot of people thinking a person with a ministry on them is mature enough to handle it. Some years ago there was a young married man that the church I was going to and had helped build up, had been bought into help with the ministry. This young guy had a great evangelistic and word of knowledge ministry. I was amazed but I had noticed some things that were not quite right. One day after he had ministered I went up to him to thank him for a good word but also to warn him about the girls. I know I went up with the right spirit, not to judge but to say just be careful, not to let your emotions get carried away. He ripped me apart and said I had no right to say anything like that to him and to mind my own business. Boy was he upset! I didn't know at the time how far he had fallen; God didn't show me that, but to warn him to be careful! I felt so strongly about it I went to see one of the older pastors (still young). He ripped me apart as well. Well I did have a right, as a father in the church, a person that had helped start the church and gone through all the hard times that had occurred with it. Paul said there is plenty of instructors in the church but not enough fathers. I know and God is my witness I was only trying to help this young man. Well he did go off into sin and possibly was at the time I challenged him, his marriage fell apart and he left the ministry. I am not sure if he's going on with the Lord today. Sad but this goes on time after time because the church oversight is too stupid to see the dangers of young people and young Christians being set up in the ministry too soon. When the church puts young people in a place of paying them to perform we also do them a disservice. If the apostle Paul worked with his hands to supply his own needs and needs of his companions, Acts 21:34, so should we in many cases. How can young people who are full time in the church find favour with God and man unless they are in the world learning to deal with the world as Christians? It is rubbish, a waste of hard earned money that people have put in to help build up the church. I have noticed over the year's churches that grow and the money comes in, the oversight seems to do ok as far as their needs being met. I feel they rely more on this than God and they lose reality with the people they are supposed to be shepherding! I was discussing this with a brother in the church a while back. I was telling him the senior pastor (for want of a better word) of a rather large Australian church was earning every year, possibly more today. It was far in excess of most people. The bloke I was talking to said he felt anybody that ran or started a corporation that size needs to have that sort of income. The church is not a corporation and I don't believe should be run like one, the church is not a one man band show. Unfortunately this is one reason why many start off ok then fail, and when they do fail they fail big time. (Many Christians don't like to hear or read about this type of thing, they can't handle it or give some lame excuse why it happened, I believe they don't know the word of God well enough, and I also believe God is exposing it as a warning to the church.) Jesus can forgive! I have no problem about that, but he also wants the church to be built right, with safeguards and not with a one man band in control which so many churches have today.

If you search Google on some of the blogs under David Yonggi Cho it should point out"On the 20th February 2014, David Yonggi Cho of Yoido Full Gospel Church, South Korea was found guilty of breach of trust, corruption and tax evasion and was sentenced to three years (it seems three years suspended sentence, possibly because of his age, he's 78) in prison, with a five year probation and $4.67 million US in fines. His son Hee-Jun was also sentenced to three years in prison for colluding with his father. How sad, when I read this it took me awhile to get over it. This man had done great things for his people and the church! But how could anybody be in a position in a church to rip off $12 to $20 million dollars over a period of time? Even if he founded the church and with all the amount of money coming in, God's money, people put their hard earned money in to help for the extension of Jesus' kingdom, not Yonggi Chos; there should have been far more accountability, far more safeguard against that type of thing. It seems that even some of the elders warned him to stop the corruption he had allowed himself to get involved in. I believe this type of thing does and can happen because one man has too much control! Even though Cho founded the church and when other people's money started coming in he shouldn't have been in the position to dictate where the monies went. What's that scripture? "Lead us not into temptation". The world seems to have far more wisdom in a lot of areas of money matters than much of the church. We in the New Testament church don't like to hear about this type of thing happening! Yet so much of the New Testament and also the Old warn us about it.

There is and has been a massive move of God in the Asian region, not just in South Korea over some years now. I personally believe its God's timing for the Asian area and there are some massive churches because of it. Cho would have been caught up in this move and grew a large Church! Many of these churches are underground because of the persecution in some of those countries they happen to be in, but we don't hear much about it. My father in law whom I never met because he died before I met his daughter and was quite a bit older than her mother, had been a missionary in Nanking the time when Japan invaded China just before the second world war. My wife was telling me that many Chinese folk came to the meetings the missionaries held, but not too many got really saved. They came mainly for the rice that was being handed out, the missionaries called them rice Christians, but never-the-less some made a real commitment to the Lord. Rosemary also told me that one time the Japanese were going through the city of Nanking chopping people's heads off and the Christians were downstairs in the basement praying for Gods protection. After the war when Mao Zedong took over the country he kicked out most of the missionaries. He also imprisoned many of the converts of the Lord, and many of these folk were in prison a very long time. I believed that God used this to mould a people, a people that were really sold out to him and when they got out of their incarceration, God, through them, brought in one of greatest moves of God the world has experienced.

Yonggi Cho's church would have to be the largest above ground Pentecostal church in the world, and what I can make out, up to a 1,000,000 people and yet he has fallen. Did he feel he was right in his own eyes and refused to be corrected? I don't know! Although it seems to be that way! Proverbs 28:18 (NIV), "He who walks in integrity will be delivered, but he who is perverse in his ways will fall into a pit", this money thing, prestige, large is best, etc etc. I think we in the church have had the wool in many cases pulled over our eyes. I guess it's time, just like King David, to repent and get back to the word and let God build the church! Is this why Paul set up elders, not one elder, to run the church at Ephesus and other places? The church is a body made up of many members working together to lift Jesus up to the world (submitting one to another). If Cho's church had been in the west, although I don't think he would have had a million members attending, the press would have had a field day! The Lord's name would have been dragged though the mud no end. I believe that Yonggi Cho's thinking was influenced by Oral Roberts and his prosperity gospel and if we are governed by the ways of the flesh it will eventually kill you! It doesn't matter who we are! When you see and have seen in the past the amount of ministry that has gone by the wayside, some who have come out of the church to draw away people so they would meet their lusts, not true fathers or mothers but as Paul called them savage wolves. Acts 20:29-31 (NIV) Paul says "I know that after I leave (the Ephesus Church) savage wolves will come in among you and will not spare the flock. Even from your own number men will arise and desert the truth in order to draw away disciples (Christians) after them so be on your guard. Remember that for three years I never stopped warning each of you night and day with tears". With tears for three years, how many shepherds will weep over the people they are supposed to be looking out for? Judge for yourself! For three years, not too many I would say! I love Paul's attitude toward his flock, a real father.

# 15

# Savaging the Flock

"I am not writing this to shame you but to warn you as my dear children (a father trying to correct his kids, fantastic). Even though you have ten thousand guardians (instructors) in Christ, you do not have many fathers in Christ Jesus, I became your father through the gospel therefore I urge you to imitate me (to be a father or mother in the Lord)", 1 Corinthians 4:14-16 (NIV). In my experience over 40 years in the church, I have seen situations start off not too bad but the envy thing comes into play. The father heart of God starts out okay in building a flock but starts to go out the window when the building of bigger churches comes into play. The guy down the road has a bigger church than us and we want one too. We have to keep up with the Jones' or Hillsong or Planet Shakers or someone else. What happens? The love for the people dries up and they become a commodity, someone to use, to build the big church, the mega church for us (I mean the Lord, sorry). When Paul set up elders (leaders, overseers, pastors) in the Ephesians' church, it stands out he wanted people with true father hearts, not just instructors. People that would correct and rebuke the flock when necessary but would do it in such a way that the flock would respect them and love them for helping them to grow like a true father should. Paul didn't want men that were more interested in building bigger churches (which is ok if it's in God). Men and women that didn't care about building monuments to themselves as King Saul did and he fleeced the sheep to do it. David was a man after God's heart (even though he had a lot of faults) and he bought back to Israel justice and equality, he had a father's heart. It was fathers and mothers in the Lord that helped me grow in my younger years as a Christian. We need that in the church today in a mighty way, more and more. Not so much a bunch of young people who don't understand what life is really all about, up the front doing their Pentecostal two steps and thinking they have the answers for everything. We had a young lady from the USA speak at the church I was attending. She spoke about her husband's work, which was ok, then she went on and on about how he liked Disneyland and how she was taking him there on his birthday and went into great detail how they had over the years done this type of thing. When Jesus said to Peter "feed my sheep" in John 21:15-18 Jesus started with lambs and went through to sheep meaning he wanted him to feed the flock right through from young to old. I bet you Jesus didn't mean feed them second rate feed, but the best of the feed, not a mouthful of stubble, substance with very little goodness in it. Today, we in many cases don't seem to be getting the depth of the word we did many years ago. It's more like a circus, full of entertainment and clowns. If anybody knows much about farming, the farmers try to produce the best pasture and feed for their animals so they get the best out of them, thus hopefully more profit. So it is with

God and his church he wants the best out of us, so he wants to feed us the best, not rubbish and entertainment which has come in great waves to the church, but many cannot see it.

I believe why many cannot tell what is going on in the church, and so much is not of God, is because they think we run the church the way of the world. They are not allowing Jesus to build the church and this is the only church that matters. He will build the church because He said He would so let's find out what He wants from us. Let's be like Mary and start to sit at His feet, listening! When King David tried to bring the Ark of the Covenant (presence of God) back the first time he messed up. It seemed right but cost a man his life. The second time he got it right but he had to go to the 'word' to find out God's way, the right way. We in the church need to go back to the word and find out about leadership. I have given you my view to some degree about young people and Christians in leadership and the way we are setting them up is wrong, not doing them or the congregation any favours. It so vitally important that we the church study to show ourself approved! Since being in the so called Pentecostal churches for the last 40 odd years and seeing the apparent mess-ups they get themselves into, control, legalism, money madness, setting up young people into ministry too early, etc, etc, no wonder people fall away! Now, about young people being set up to early, the church seems to justify this because what they read in 1 and 2 Timothy, that Timothy was a young man doing the work of an older man. To Paul, Timothy was a young man, but in fact he wasn't when he wrote those letters to him. Just to throw this in, as an older man, men in their forties are still classed as young to me. When Timothy meets Paul, it is estimated that Timothy was in his twenties and when he penned the letters to him, which was many years later, he could have been as old as 48 years of age. Google on to 'How old was Timothy'. I believe if our so called leaders in our so called Pentecostal churches had taken 'time out' to check the way the church should be run, we would not have the mess-ups, disapointments and hurts we have now.

I joined a church once run by three young men all married with young children. The meeting was in a school hall. The band was playing and the presence of God was very real. After the meeting I was standing talking to an older chap who has become a very good friend, his name is John Fletcher, whom has helped me a lot over the years! As we were talking a young kid ran past very distraught crying out that two of the pastors were getting rid of the other pastor. This shocked me, so I asked my friend about it, he said it was true and I asked why. He said that the pastor that was asked to leave didn't fit into the vision that the other two had in mind. Having been through so much of this thing before and seeing the harm it does to the flock, it concerned me no end. Here were three young men who had together wanted to do something for God, started a church. No doubt they all had some sort of ministry, zealous but without much wisdom or knowledge. It would have been a big high at the beginning, then the realities of life hit them later. It's like marriage, at the beginning it's a honeymoon or more of infatuation, then you start to find out what the other person is really like and sometimes you start to think what have I done, but children have come along. "I feel trapped, let me out of here" (well some do). As we well know

God hates (hate is a strong word but it leaves no doubt) divorce.

Over the years what I have noticed and have been through myself is break ups in church. To younger Christians it can be devastating, so it is in the marriage. The world may say it doesn't have a long term effect on children but in what I have come across that is utter bull, it does. Paul set standards for oversight of churches because he wanted people that really loved the flock, who through their own experience of life knew how to bring up a family who in turn loved and respected the parents. So much in the church today miss the mark and I really believe it is because we don't know the word well enough. I believe many so called oversights of churches do not understand their responsibility either. These young ministers really didn't have a clue of the harm they were doing. Yes they could have callings on their lives but zealousness without wisdom or knowledge is not good, as the scripture states. The minister that was asked to leave didn't do it right away and the situation got to me because of what I had seen and gone through myself in the past. I made an appointment to see the ministers separately I felt so strongly about it. I had come to know these guys quite well over the time I was there. They didn't agree with my point of view. I said that God didn't agree with what they were doing either but I don't think they believed me. I left the meeting feeling nothing was accomplished but we still stayed friends. The other minister left and the church did what churches do. After a while I felt I couldn't stay there any longer. I had to cry out to God if it was me, did I get my nose out of joint about what I said and them not accepting it, was I out of place and needed correction. This happened over a couple of months and I couldn't find any peace, in fact it got worse. I said to Rosemary that I had to leave or at least not go to the Sunday meetings. Rosemary didn't say much but she took the kids there over the three years I didn't go. I had got to know some of the older people there. They had a get together, a cell group type thing which I used to go to. I also went, at times, to another church. I was into wild pig hunting at the time and with my two dogs, did a lot of it. It's wonderful how God works. He used this time to calm my spirit down and have time out with him. I would go out by myself a lot of the time and to be in the outdoors was great. It was how I was bought up in New Zealand.

At home we never talked about how the church was going and I heard through the grapevine that the services had doubled and had started a night service. Did I make a blue? I was also concerned with my kids, with me not being at church. I asked my son when he was older if he thought I was going away from God. He said "no dad, not at all I see you reading your Bible and praying" as I had always done. After about three years I felt the Lord speaking to my heart about going back. I said "Lord, I can't, how will they receive me". I was starting to think that I had made a blue and was wrong. The call to go back got stronger and stronger, so I did. I took a young bloke that I had met and become friends with. I went to the night service which I thought would be packed but it wasn't. Still I enjoyed the service. After a short time of going back the senior pastor (want of a better word) and I became quite close and would often meet for coffee and a chat now and then. The fact I hadn't been to his church for about three years was never discussed, he had too many other things on his mind. The poor guy was carrying a real heavy load on his shoulders.

The church after I had left had shot ahead, numbers increased until it was overflowing, but something was not right. You know the bible says that unless the house is built right it will not stand. Whatever we do for the kingdom must be done God's way, not our way. People started to leave in numbers and there were bleating sheep all over the place. As I said previously, my family and I never talked about what was happening in the church. I didn't know that the church was going through a hard time. The pastor and I would chat and at times he would ask me about things relating to the church and what was going on and I didn't really know what he was talking about. On our last get together over coffee I asked him what he thought God was up to. Like me he wasn't sure, so we left it at that. Leaving I went back to my office and just sat down and the presence of God hit me like a ton of bricks. The Lord spoke to my spirit that He was going to bring in a new wine, a new moving of God. But first he had to get rid of the old wine skin and you don't sew a new patch on a rotting garment. God was replacing the old for the new so it could carry and reflect what God was about to do in the church. The old wine skin and garments were not good enough. I took it that this was what he was doing in the church or going to do. I rang the pastor to tell him what I felt God was going to do but he wasn't there. He rang me back the next morning and I told him what had happened the day before. He went very quiet but didn't say much. He got back to me a couple of days later and told me that at the previous Sunday night service, which I didn't go to, a chap had come up to him, who wasn't a member of our church, I didn't know him from a bar of soap and to this day still don't, had told him almost word for word what I had said later on. The pastor had felt he should step down and let someone else take over. This was before he got the word that I had said I felt from the Lord. He told his wife what the first bloke had said and she said 'no way', they had just bought a new house and had just moved into it. Then a few days later I came along and put the spanner in the works, the wife agreed that it was from the Lord for them and later on they left. I admired that bloke because he was humble enough to see all was not right and he didn't have the calling to fix it. He went to another church and as far as I know he is doing a great job. From time to time we chat on the phone. It wasn't long after the situation that I lost my wife to cancer. The pastor's wife was absolutely fantastic and so was the church. The way they conducted the service and meal afterwards was fabulous. Thanks again folks. It really took a load off me. We had a caretaker pastor until the new bloke came in. The caretaker pastor did an unbelievable job under very difficult circumstances, good one brother Benny Bishop. Even though the pastor that moved on thought the word was for him and his situation, I felt and still believe, it was for the church overall. I was staying at a friend's house not too much later on and they had a Christian channel on which I don't have at home. I was watching this and almost word for word someone said they really believed that God was going to do a new thing to take the church on to a greater place in him but the old wine skin and garment could not handle this so God was replacing them with new ones.

I really believe that God has order and he will bring the church back to this. Unfortunately we all have a problem, we are at times entrenched in something or way of thinking and is hard to shift but I believe God has a way. When King David sinned with Bathsheba and killed her husband I guess he thought he had got away with it. Now if one of the ordinary folk had come up to him and told him his problem, he probably would have had their head chopped off. God used a prophet to do the job; he had the anointing to carry the word to David and because King David had a great love for God, repented right away. It took a prophet to change his thinking to go on with God and I believe God will rise up prophets to change the thinking of the church so the glory of God can come back in a way we have not seen before. How many times have we seen great men of God possessing the land for God only to see wild beast come in and almost destroy the work. I believe God is going to bring in the word to help the church safeguard against this type of thing. We must take time out to hear what the Spirit is saying to the churches. Unfortunately a lot of churches have so much going on that people don't have time to really study the word for themselves and just go along with what the pastors say. The bible does say don't let anybody teach you, allow the Holy Spirit to do that. If something is of God, ok, accept it, if not, reject it. Don't go along with something just because some high powered preacher says so, check it out, and this can take time being with the Lord by yourself! God is looking for true worshipers in spirit and in truth not by the whim of the flesh, which I believe so much of the church is built on.

# 16

# Learning To Tell the Difference

At the beginning of this book, I stated that at one of the first meetings I had ever attended, the preacher said that Christians should pay tithe on the amount before tax is taken out and was quite adamant about it and I felt there was something wrong with that doctrine. That preacher was Frank Houston from New Zealand, from a church not far from where I came from in NZ. In the early seventies my wife and I went over there to stay with my folks for about 10 months as Dad had some townhouses he wanted me to help build and we attended Houston's church. I thought the church ok but thought Frank at times was a bit of a showman. We didn't know that he was involved in paedophilia which was bought out later on but almost covered up. Since then other situations of paedophilia and other sexual activities have been brought to bear. Frank Houston is the founder or one of the founders of Hillsong church in Sydney. Jesus said in Matthew 7:15- 23 (NIV), verse15, watch out for false prophets, they come to you in sheep's clothing but inwardly they are ferocious wolves, verse 16, by their fruit you will recognise them. Do people pick grapes from thornbushes, or figs from thistles? verse 17, likewise every good tree bears good fruit but a bad tree bears bad fruit, verse 18, a good tree cannot bear bad fruit and a bad tree cannot bear good fruit, verse 19, every tree that does not bear good fruit is cut down and thrown into the fire, verse 20, thus by their fruit you will recognise them, verse 21, not everyone who says to me "Lord, Lord who will enter the kingdom of heaven, but only he who does the will of my Father who is in heaven", verse 22, many will say to me on that day "Lord. Lord did we not prophesy in your name, and in you name drive out demons and perform many miracles!" verse 23, then I will tell them plainly, I never knew you, away from me you evil doers.

Many in the church do not realise that ministry gifts are not the fruit of the Holy Spirit. Jesus brings this out in Matthew. Over the years many men and woman have through their ministry done great things. They have used the gift of ministry God has given them and by faith moved mountains, set up great works etc but in the end crashed and burned. Some of these people even raised up worldwide denominations and works. Sad, but it's a fact and we need to know and understand the difference between gifts of the spirit and fruit of the spirit. The letter to Philemon, a Christian slave owner whom Paul stayed with at times, shows us some of the fruit of the spirit. Paul was in prison in Rome or Ephesus for his faith. Onesimus, a slave of Philemon, had apparently stolen from his master and ran away to find Paul. For a slave to run away, under the Roman law was punishable by death. I surmise that Onesimus had met Paul on one of his stays with Philemon, possibly heard from Philemon where Paul was in prison and decided to find him out. There was something that he found favour with in Paul. He found him and became a Christian through Paul's ministry. I wonder if Onesimus had stolen from his master so he could survive his journey (I guess we will never know). Anyway he was willing to return to his master. Paul knew that the master wouldn't be too happy about what this slave had done so he wrote him a letter appealing to his Christian mind and emotions, to accept Onesimus as a brother in Christ and not just as a bit of property that deserved death. Paul was also willing to pay back himself what Onesimus had stolen even though he wasn't quite sure how much. This was a true heart of a father being manifested through Paul. People to him were not a numbers game or a commodity to build up his mega church. Think about it a moment Paul didn't really know how much was stolen, so in a sense was taking a big risk by offering to pay back the amount. Read through the letter to Philemon yourself, shortest book in the bible so shouldn't take too long to see the heart of Paul, quite amazing. This is what God the father is looking for in the church, true worshipers, in spirit and in truth. There is nothing wrong with the gifts of the Spirit. Jesus himself used them and drew great crowds, did great miracles, but like the ten lepers only one was thankful that Jesus healed him.

There has been and still is an emphasis on the gifts, power, miracles etc and yet Jesus was more interested in the fruit of the Spirit which brings us to a closer relationship to him, a love relationship with him, like a married couple, to be one flesh, where we know him intimately. In the Song of Solomon it teaches us what really brings forth the best of fruits that God is looking for. "Awake north wind (dry, hot wind) and come, south wind (wet, cold wind) blow on my garden that its fragrance may flow out, let my lover come into His garden and taste its choice fruits", Song of Solomon 4:16 (NIV). It's as we go through times that seem dry and hot, times that things seem to dry up in our life. Nothing is going to plan, almost like we are going backwards. Times when things seem frosty, nothing seems to be growing; everything has come to a standstill. Real hard, tough times when extremes hit us like a ton of bricks and it's like we cannot stand the extremes that confront us. Its times when we want to throw up our hands and say 'enough is enough'. It's times like these where we cry out to God to help us through the night. Its times like these that our help comes from above, to rely on Jesus to get us through it. Its times like these that he sends the rain in our hearts and lives that produces the fruit He is looking for. I believe our love relationship with Him is more important than all the faith we have to prophesy in His name, to drive out demons or perform many miracles and build big buildings. God is looking for the fragrance of a love relationship produced through the winds of hard times to spread abroad that others may see Christ in us, not of ourselves, lest we boast about it. I believe God wants to take the church on to a greater holiness wanting to get rid of the old wine skin and garment to replace them with new ones so as to handle the new outpouring of his revelation that he wants to pour into the church. I believe that there hasn't been enough accountability over the years and God will restore this lack. When we look back over the years of men and women that have built churches, just in Australia and New Zealand as well as in the USA and Britain that have gone and got involved in scandals. It is no small thing.

Clark Taylor, who had one of the biggest churches in Australia for some time but couldn't keep his hands off the ladies, Neville Johnson, who for a season ran the largest Pentecostal church in Australasia, a man that believed he had special grace from God to engage in affairs over several years until those involved came forward, but Johnson refused to be corrected. He was so caught up in his own deception as a chosen 'one of God'.

Frank Houston, who I spoke of before, confessed to the sexual abuse of young (under age) males in his New Zealand congregation, possibly about the time my wife and I were attending his church. No wonder I felt he was a bit off, a showman at times. Something didn't feel right with his ministry. Neville Johnson had a big influence on my life as well as others. He was a great teacher but again in my spirit something didn't feel quite kosher and God released me from this later on. Growing up in the Lord we were taught "don't touch God's anointed", meaning to say any one that seems to be doing great things for the Lord shouldn't be criticised or pulled down. Now the scriptures do say to respect leaders but respect is something you earn. I believe that under the Old Testament the king was top dog, he was God's man for the hour. Jesus completely turned this around and said the last shall be first. Unfortunately we judge things the world's way. We are all priests and kings, the whole lot of us and Jesus warned those that cause any of the young ones to fall (young Christians). It's better to have a mill stone around their neck and thrown into the sea than have the wrath of God come after them. When I look back over the years and contemplate on what has been, when I think of what has happened in the church, of how many in my small circle I know of have had a great effect on me and my thinking, then having to turn around later on in life to change my attitudes. Men like Houston, Taylor, Johnson, Baker (Perth) and Jimmy Swaggart, I used to rush home from church to watch him on TV until he crashed. He still didn't seem to learn from it! Jim and Tammy Bakker, to name a very few, the list goes on and on. These people have been put up on a pedestal and almost, if not worshiped like Gods. Today we have TV evangelists as well as some churches that command this type of thing and young Christians and immature Christians who don't know any better flock to them. People that have a responsibility to feed the sheep that they minister to but so much of the time there is more fleecing of the flock, so they can have their lavish lifestyle, palatial mansions, jet planes and big expenses accounts, all in the name of Jesus, of course it is. Maybe I'm naive but my God hasn't led me that way. Yes we all make mistakes and if we really repent "God forgives us", thank God. It's all about keeping our relationship right with God and building on it. When we see the scandals that have occurred over the years I would say that many of these folks didn't and many of them carry on in the same sin! Now to be fair, Jimmy Bakker got caught out in a sex scandal which led to the resignation of his ministry and a subsequent revelation of accounting fraud landed him in jail and brought about his divorce from his then wife Tammy. I thank God for his mercies, because as much as I can make out, Jimmy repented of his ways, came back to the Lord and spending the next five years locked up had time to study the Bible! Since his release, he seems to have gone all out preaching against the prosperity gospel that many are involved in and he himself was truly caught up with. We do not have enough accountability in the church. It's not a one man band, its submitting one to another. Jesus didn't do anything unless he knew what the Father God approved first. The Father, Son and Holy Spirit work together in harmony, in unity and that's where God commanded the blessing. Today and it has been for some time, we have one man (and women) band ministry and I believe this is one of the reasons why so many go off the rails. If they allowed God to point out what is in their hearts they would see and act on situations that lead to trouble. A lot of it has to do with pride, agendas, control, legalism, money, sex, etc. I believe that the Lord will become the Lord of the Church and He is and will deal with the rot. We blame the Catholic Church for cover ups regarding scandals in their church, but I feel this is just as bad in the Pentecostal church. When I see the Frank Houston situation of paedophilia and he confessed it, how come he didn't go to jail? We are all under the law of the land; in fact, Paul used it to his own advantage when he needed to.

Leadership everywhere brings responsibility, especially in the church. This is why we must submit to the leading of the Holy Spirit. Jesus said His way is easy if we learn to submit our way to Him. The more we die to 'self' the better off we are. When Jesus came He was looking for the fruit and He gave the illustration of the fig tree. It had plenty of leaves, it looked good, but didn't have any fruit and He cursed it. This was an illustration of what Israel was up to, plenty of religion but no true heart relationship with God, no fruit. So much of it shows us what is going on in the church today. We must, just like King David did to bring back the Ark of the Covenant, the presence of God the right way, wait on God and get back to his word. When Jesus looked for fruit on the fig tree, he didn't find any, and he cursed it! The 'Song of Solomon' teach us the way how fruit is produced to bring out the best yield. It is a book of love and what love goes through to produce the best love. It is about a husband and his wife and the intimacy of that relationship to bring them to a greater love relationship with one another; so it is also with the church. The heart of God sent Jesus into the world to die for our sin and through faith we accept this but we must all go on to a greater maturity in Him to produce the fruit He is looking for.

Jesus at the fig tree was looking for fruit, not gifts. Many people of God have experienced great gifts of the Holy Spirit, done great things for God (read God's Generals by Robert Liardon) but have gone off the rails, why? I believe they were more interested in their gift and not their relationship with their true God. We often read about business men and women, sports people, people who have done great things according to this world's standard but their marriage relations have fallen apart. The relationships with their children, wife and friends etc have been shipwrecked because they didn't take time out to build the more important thing in their lives. I believe this kind of thing is going on in the church. Paul saw this same thing going on in the early church and said "there are ten thousand instructors but very few fathers; I will be a father to you". It gets back to a father-child relationship, a husband-wife relationship as in the book of Song of Solomon; the whole bible is about a true relationship with our God. He has saved us, but now he wants to kill us so the flesh will have no part in the glory that is before us. We must reckon ourselves dead to the old life and go on from glory to glory in Him. Jesus said "The gates of hell will not prevail against the church He is building but, and I mean but, will prevail against the church we try to build in the flesh". Just like the apostle Paul, submitted himself back to the other apostles to check out his doctrine and the way of doing things, so we must submit ourselves to others to check ourselves out. It is God's way of doing things and a safeguard for the church. It is not about covering ourselves with 'yes men' but people that can correct and rebuke in love if need be. Jesus is indeed building his church and we must be willing to hear what the spirit is saying to the churches.

In the book of Revelation 2:1-7 (RSV) God commends the church in Ephesus for the good things they had done thus far. The hard work they had put in and they had persevered at it and when false apostles had come along, they dealt with them no end. The apostle Paul had warned them big time about these people in the church that would draw away Christians after themselves to control, dictate over, fleece, etc. and in many cases build their own monuments. People that could have started off ok but along their Christian growth their own egos kicked in and not allowing God to deal with it went on from one deception to another. This can happen to all of us if we don't allow God to deal with it. We must continually submit to God and His ways. I am convinced that one of the safeguards we have in our Christian walk, if not the greatest, is our first love for the Lord. The church in Ephesus had abandoned this and God was telling them to get back to it or he would remove their anointing. God wants intimacy with

His people and he wants it to grow with true worshipers in spirit and in truth.

The apostle Paul tells in Philippians 2:12&13 (NIV) "Therefore, my dear friends (father's heart) as you have always obeyed, not only in my presence, but now much more in my absence (this letter was sent from prison) continue to work out your salvation with fear and trembling, for it is God who works in you to will (his will) and to act according to his good purpose". Today the fear of God seems, in many cases, to have gone out the window. We seem to think that we can do what we like and get away with it, but we can't. God will not be mocked! The grace of God is not a licence to sin, as a friend of mine, a man that really loves the Lord, pointed out. It's there to help us repent if we do sin and all of us do at times. It is there to express the father heart of God, but also to show us that God is a righteous and just God who will not put up with our nonsense for too long. He will expose it as he did with David and Bathsheba and with Ananias and Sapphira in the book of Acts! Ecclesiastes 12:14 (NIV) "For God will bring every deed into judgement including every hidden thing, whether it is good or evil". Sometimes he does it right away and sometimes over time.

When you think about how we in the church have been hoodwinked by 'false apostles'; how we have allowed them to dictate how the church is run, only to build their own monuments for their own glory. I think of men like Frank Houston, one of the founders of Hillsong church in Sydney, I believe, and is the largest attended church in Australia. Frank is deceased and the church is run by his son Brian Houston. Frank Houston was a

New Zealander and was a very prominent member of the New Zealand Assembly of God. Frank, a very charismatic man, was their superintendent and senior pastor of the Assembly of God church in Lower Hutt, (NZ) which he founded. My wife and I attended Frank's church in 1972/73 for ten months before we came back to Perth. In the time we were there I felt something wasn't quite kosher, but I didn't know what. The church seemed to run along quite well, great singing and the preaching was okay but at times I thought Frank was a bit of a showman. At the time I thought maybe I had a bit of a critical spirit but if a man acts like a clown what are you supposed to think. While we were there I can't remember any accusation of paedophilia coming to light, just something didn't sit right. When Rosemary and I returned to Perth, my spirit couldn't find peace about Frank. I saw him preach in Perth some years later and my attitude toward him didn't change. The first time I had any idea about sexual misconduct relating to Frank was when I received an open letter from someone accusing him of being involved in such conduct. I was absolutely shocked and didn't know what to believe or think. It seemed so outrageous and unbelievable. The letter now is lost so I can't quite remember the full content. This was before other accusations started to come to light sometime later. When they did come to light an investigation was ordered by the Hillsong church and it seems also the Assemblies of God church in Australia. The investigation was conducted by a Pastor John Lewis, who found the allegations were true. When you log onto the internet and search Pastor Frank Houston, Part 1, Paedophile Activities, it seems the paedophile allegations go back to the 1960s right through to the 1980s and beyond! Frank was not only involved in paedophile activity, which is bad enough, but also homo-erotic activity when he came to Australia, the man is nothing more than a pervert of the highest order. After going through much of the stuff on the internet about Frank Houston you could make a film about him. (Mind you, who would want to see it?)

Over the years I came to realise the church of Jesus Christ contains evil people that want to be up front, who love to lead, who want to build a name for themselves, who are driven by a wrong spirit, the devil comes as an angel of light, and we must be on guard. As far as I can make out Brian Houston, Hillsong Movement, and Assemblies of God will not release the official A.O.G. report on Frank Houston and his sinful activities. They seem to have tried to sanitise and reinvent the life of this man, making out he did fall but it was only about once. As we go through the blogs there were many people involved and possibly others that have not come forward. Sad that this man could have had so much control over other people, ruining so many lives! The bible warns us about these people and we should expose them. They are evil people that do not care about others, only about their perverted desires, being evil to the core. No wonder Paul calls these people "savage wolves". Knowing the church that Hillsong is, I can understand not wanting to make a big song and dance about Frank. It's a church that brings in, according to a report on T.V. on or about March 2015, thereabouts of $72 million dollars every year, all in the name of Jesus. What Jesus are they talking about? Maybe it's about serving the money Jesus who will so easily turn us away from the true Jesus; you know the one in the bible!

When I first heard Frank in 1969, he stated that tithing should be conducted before tax. I mentioned about this at the start of the book. Well folks, I don't tithe because of my understanding of what Jesus did on the cross. He fulfilled all, all, all of the requirements of the law. I, as much as I know how, allow Jesus to teach me how I should give through His Word and Spirit. Many churches, not just Hillsong, teach on tithing as almost a law. Why? They are too scared not to; they really don't know how to trust God to provide for their needs, thinking the more money they bring in the greater they stand before God! Some ministers need to get off their after thoughts and work for a living as Paul did when need be. I believe that Jesus wants a 100% of us and we must be open to hear what the Spirit is saying to our hearts! Now, if a person wants to tithe, let them do it. It's between them and their God! To say that people should tithe before tax or to have to tithe at all is rubbish; nonsense, to make a law out of it is so wrong! My Jesus fulfilled the Law! I'm not too sure about your Jesus? Maybe he's the money Jesus or the pride of life Jesus that so many deceived preachers preach about today! Why is it that churches teach that circumcision, going to church on Saturday, keeping the Sabbath day holy, keeping feast days, animal sacrifices, among other things, not eating a calf boiled in its mother's milk (could never work that one out), is not necessary to keep because Jesus fulfilled them on the cross and they are right, but tithing, you don't touch the sacred cow, heck NO. How do we keep our mega churches going, keep me in a job and give me a very good wage. Warning: If you are going to live by one part of the law you must live by all of it. It's unfortunate that many churches teach tithing as a law or almost a law and over the years I have heard so much on tithe and giving it's no wonder that many churches don't know really what it is all about.

Paul looks at the church as a family run by a father's heart. Paul with his father's heart explains it this way in 2 Corinthians 12:14 "Now I am ready to visit you for the third time and I will not be a burden to you because what I want is not your possessions but you". Paul was not someone who wanted their money to build his empire, or make a name for himself, exploit and use people as commodities for his own ends! Hey hang on we need money to keep the ship going. I could not agree more but not the controlling way many of the churches teach. After all, the Lord loves a cheerful giver! I also believe that if someone goes to a church and they feel it's the right one for them, being fed the word etc, then they should give for the running of the place, but it's up to them how much! Paul goes on to say as we read in verse 14 "after all, children should not have to save up for their parents, but parents for their children. So I will very gladly spend for you everything I have and expand myself as well". The whole chapter should be read! Again the true heart of God is expressed through Paul, a man that died to 'self'. To say that I'm against giving would be wrong; the bible teaches us we should. Nobody knows how much I give, it's between me and God. I believe many people are too scared not to tithe, because over the years they have been so indoctrinated to do it and believe if they don't, they are robbing God and he wants to bless them; under the Old Testament that would have been true, under law yes, but we are not under law but under grace and truth in our Lord Jesus Christ. Paul writing to the Galatians' church was trying to correct them because some Jewish Christians had come in and told them that much of the Old Testament was binding and the Galatians had to keep it. He explained to the Galatians that they had come out of bondage of worshiping false Gods (they were pagan) and were falling back into slavery by allowing themselves to put into practice some of the Old Jewish law! Paul goes on to explain that the law was to lead the Jews to Christ, to be justified by faith and not by the supervision of the law! Galatians 3:24 and Galatians 4:8-10 (NIV) tells us some of the things that the Galatians were doing was observing special days, months, seasons and years. Also they were keeping the law of circumcision, as Paul brings out in Galatians 5:11&12.(NIV) He was so upset by those jokers that were trying to bring in 'justification through law' he said they should go the whole hog and not only circumcise, but castrate themselves as well! (Good one Paul, I really like that bloke). Not long ago, a church I was attending had a new pastor come in and take over. He was a strong willed, gifted and a charismatic young man. It wasn't long before he was showing DVDs on tithing to the church on Sundays and not only then but they had to be shown to the midweek meetings as well! This minister used to say and possibly still does that the tithe belongs to God! Under the Old law, the one that Jesus fulfilled, that would have been so, and he is right, but who wants to live under that law? The law of rules and regulations, which the Old Testament people couldn't keep anyway! Thank God for Jesus and what he did on the cross! The guy that was presenting tithing in the DVD was so far off; I reckon that he would have had trouble finding his way home! God help us all. It was nothing but legalism to the core! The young minister, who allowed this rubbish to be shown, really doesn't understand what Gods intentions for the church are, even though he's gifted in many areas and has a head understanding of scripture, this in itself does not make him a leader in God's kingdom, his own maybe but not the lords. He quite clearly doesn't know that Jesus has fulfilled all the law and brought in grace and truth with a father's heart! The truth of scripture is not put into practise because so much of the church has been taught wrong and many ministers think they are doing the right thing, but so much of it does not line up with the word of God, the Spirit of God, the nature of God and what Jesus did on the cross. So much of this false teaching is running a muck in so many churches today! Let me ask you something, the church, is it built on money or a true father's heart? If it is by the heart of the father then why isn't it put to practise in the church? Not by this controlling, legalistic and down right money hungry wolves that are building up their own glory, thinking they are doing God's will! I believe that so much of the church everywhere, has been so wrongly taught about how to grow the church, the system of the world has come in and taught without fleecing money out of the congregation all the time, its not God's will. I was talking to a friend yesterday and he told me that a person he knew had left that church (Kingdom City WA) because all they talked about was money. (For of the abundance of the heart his mouth speaketh) Luke 6:45 (KJV). The so called shepherd's will say they are not fleecing the flock, but building the Lord's kingdom and they need money to do it, look what they are doing for the Lords kingdom! I would say to them that so much is not the Lords kingdom they are building but their own!

You know, the Catholic church does a lot of good works as well, they build schools, hospitals, places for wayward kids, drug rehabilitation centres etc and so far as I can make out so does the Mormon Church, and God bless them for that! Yet when I was in the Catholic Church all those years ago, I felt something missing, I was never taught that the way of salvation was though Jesus Christ, salvation was through their church, and I was a Catholic so I was ok! The Spirit of God who brings in truth and the true father heart was missing to a large degree, it was just a religion and I found Jesus outside that church later on! It must break the father heart of God when he sees the way much of what we humans have tried to build His church, by our flesh and the way of the world. Now, to be fair the Lord is doing a real work in both those churches and has his people that love him and are serving him with the knowledge they have. Remember in God's house there are many mansions! It's Jesus that saves, not churches; I myself was outside the church when I got saved. Today there are churches that also teach that we need to keep Saturday (the Sabbath) as the right day of worship, again legalism, well I don't know about your Jesus but my Jesus is greater than that and I believe every days a good day to worship my Lord! By the way if they want to worship on Saturday, do it, but treat it as a law? Watch out, else it will bind you up; as tithing does too many Christians today because of the way they have been wrongly taught!

# 17

# Be Careful What Spirit Controls You

In life people can say things that can be really hurtful, now it's up to us if we accept the words spoken or not. In some of the blogs on Frank Houston from Hillsong church it is said that Frank as a young man was told over and over again that he would not amount to much in life. Now, when I was in Frank's church in NZ between 1972/73 I heard him talk about this many times and it seemed he was almost controlled by it! It was his teacher by all accounts that said this to him and I believe Frank took this to heart and it got to him. He built up a resolve; I believe to prove the teacher wrong. It is my opinion that Frank never forgave that person and what he said. This thing grew and grew until it became a driving force in Frank's life and nobody better get in the way. Jesus said I will build the church and not the flesh of man. I believe Frank used the church to fulfill his ambitions to become a somebody, at least in his own eyes. Unfortunately he has dragged others along with him, the blind leading the blind as the saying goes. It was in the 1970s that the wicked allegations about Frank started to surface. This was in Lower Hutt Assembly of God, NZ. When challenged about it, he lost the plot. Woe-betide that anybody challenged

Frank about anything. He seems to have suppressed the allegations and I believe some of his associates and lay leaders left his service. It has come to the surface years later that the allegations were true. Frank was a very evil and crafty man, which paedophiles are. I believe that Frank, because of his wounded spirit, regarding the not amounting to anything comments, clouded his relationship with the Lord and it took over. He had a foul temper and a foul treatment of leaders who he didn't like, or who opposed or challenged him in anyway. Google search Pastor Frank Houston Part 2 and 5. Frank was known in NZ as 'Cranky Frank'. Frank is typical of paedophiles, which have an evil spirit in my opinion; same as those involved in homosexual activities, they are unnatural and evil according to the bible. Paedophiles love to control weak people, people that are vulnerable. I believe Frank was controlled by an evil spirit and loved to be first, to control, to be the man. Jesus said in the kingdom that first shall be last. Frank never humbled himself before the Lord. He was a very, very evil man and the hurt he caused and damage done is unthinkable and yet he is still honoured by some today. I am convinced that much of his ministry was governed by "the power of positive thinking" or blab it and grab it, type ministry.

    I remember watching TV one night and it was about honouring Darren Beadman, the well known Australian jockey. Frank Houston was asked to say a few words about Darren. As far as I can make out Frank had led him to the Lord. Frank went on about how God would use Darren in some type of ministry to lead others to the Lord etc, you know "big time", it's always "big time". Again in my spirit I felt warning bells. If you Google search "Darren Beadsman faith" and read "Thy word is a lamp to my feet" the DB debacle by Hughie Seaborn, you can make up your own mind. We are living in days of great deception and as Christians we need to live very close to the Lord, continuously making Him Lord. Day by day, work out our salvation in fear and trembling. The thing that kept me close to my wife, who has gone to be with the Lord, was the word of God and leading and guidance of the Holy Spirit.

My love for my wife got stronger through very trying times by "committing our ways unto the Lord" and allowing God to deal with us when need be. There were times that I would look at Rosemary and I thought that my heart was going to burst through my ribcage because of my love for her. I would think to myself that I could never do anything that would harm her and regret later on! It would affect her too much! This got stronger as the years progressed. So it is with God he wants our love and devotion in a very real and strong way! I don't think he's that interested in fair weather friends! When we put ourselves last and him first, putting aside our flesh and the corrupt things that go along with it, we get closer to him. Intermittently I don't believe Frank Houston had that love for God because how could he do what he did over and over it seems, maybe even longer than thirty years or more, until he was found out? When you blog onto the many accusations about Frank it seems he was challenged in the 1970s but denied them. King David when pointed out his sin by the prophet, repented right away. He did this when the lord revealed other sins in his life as well. I believe he did this because of his relationship with his God which I don't believe Frank had and

I believe there are many in ministry and the church like it today.

I am not going to give my judgement on Frank and where he ends up, but he has been honoured by some so called prominent Christians! Blog on to Christian Witness Ministries, written by Mark Mullins. Let me ask you something, did Judas get honoured in scripture or dishonoured? He ended up spilling his guts all over the place. He's known as a traitor. Judas was one of the twelve apostles and did great signs and wonders but had something wrong in his heart which he never allowed God to deal with. He was a crook and a turncoat and he is a warning for others to take note of. In the book of Acts there is another couple that we need to look at as a warning not to mess with God. Galatians 6:7 "God cannot be mocked". Ananias and Sapphira were early Christians who thought they could pull the wool over the Holy Spirit, big note themselves and lied to God about how much money they got for some land which they sold and gave to the church. Is the Bible honouring them for the evil they did? No, it's written as a warning to others.

The Christian Witness Ministries 'Honouring the late Frank Houston', my question is, should guys like Frank Houston be honoured anyway? NO and yet he was and is still honoured to some degree now. His past as a paedophile and involvement in homo-erotic activities are watered down so much that Brian Houston and Hillsong bring it out that way, to try and get people to believe that Frank did fall into paedophilia but only once over 30 odd years or so. A paedophile, in records, does not shake that sin off easily overnight. Frank did his evil deeds in New Zealand and carried them over to Australia when he came over here. Some of his evil deeds were even published in newspapers and yet he was honoured. How far has the church gone off the rails?

Jesus gives us stern warnings about the sin of association and by honouring someone we are saying we agree with what they did, their evil ways; if that is what they did? Matthew 23:29 "Woe to you, teachers of the law and Pharisees, you hypocrites! You build tombs for the prophets and decorate the graves of the righteous. And you say 'If we had lived in the days of our forefathers, we would not have taken part with them in shedding the blood of the prophets'. So you testify against yourselves, that you are the descendant of those who murdered the prophets, fill up then, the measure of the sin in your forefathers." So the same rule applies when we honour someone, we agree with what they did. Frank should not be honoured in any way, shape or form; by their fruits you will know them. This is like the world we live in; the criminals seem to get the praises and the victims pushed to one side, told to shut their mouths and don't complain. In the US military a dishonourable discharge once handed down is considered the most reprehensible of conduct. All veterans' benefits are lost regardless of any past honourable service. This type of discharge is regarded as shameful in the military, and so it should be in the church. No honour was given to Judas or Ananias and Sapphira, but a warning to the church that we must allow God to deal with our sin. This is not a speck or even a plank in one's eye. This is gross misconduct that can dishonour God's name. The church is not there to GLORIFY MAN but is there to GLORIFY GOD. Leaders in the church have a great responsibility to be without fault and again I'm talking about situations that can and do bring dishonour to the Lord's name, not just a speck or even a plank! I emailed Brian Houston for a copy of the report on Frank Houston done by Pastor John Lewis but no reply. Ok, I am nobody, I didn't really expect one but I tried. The fact is there seems to be a cover up on Frank's past and I have already given my view. I also believe that the New Zealand A.O.G. should have dealt more diligently with the allegations that were cast against Frank Houston right back in the 1970s. If that had happened, it could have possibly saved much heartache for people caught up with Frank later on. If it was exposed then he should have got out the ministry, thus stopping the leaven permeating though so much of the church. Look at the early church, they didn't muck around when gross sin was committed and we are not dealing with a young Christian here! All sin is wrong and needs to be dealt with and the sin of paedophiles is some thing even our lax society will not accept!

NEWS FLASH    NEWS FLASH

In 2014 a royal commission on child sex abuse in Australia was conduced, and as far as I can make out, still is. Brian Houston from Hillsong church was called to give evidence why the church didn't report their knowledge about Frank Houston's involvement in such behaviour. The Daily Telegraph in Sydney published in print on 7th October 2014 much of what was said at the commission. Hillsong would have known about Frank's misdeeds on or before early 2000 and the church did sack Frank from preaching, but Frank was never reported to the police. The paper goes on to say that up to 50 pastors of the Assemblies of God in the 1970s from his native land of New Zealand knew of allegations that he touched the genitalia of 6 boys right back then, again as far as I can make out, not reported. Oh church how far we have fallen! I believe that Brian Houston, after his part of the commission hearing was concluded, got up in front of his mega church and apologised to the congregation for not reporting to the police about Frank when the evidence against him was too strong for Hillsong and others to deny or cover up. Again, as far as I can ascertain the congregation stood up and clapped and cheered Brian. I bet that was some show put on by Brian, and it would have taken hours to clean up the mess of all the used tissues. I personally believe that Hillsong knew about Frank's paedophile misdeeds before the early 2000s because they go right back to the 1970s, as brought out in the Royal Commission. People have said to me that Frank was Brian's father and would have found it hard to report him to the police. This may seem to have some bearing on why he didn't, but I don't believe it one little bit. It was said that good old Brian slammed his old man "as repulsive" at the commission. Brian and Hillsong church had their backs to the wall when the truth came out. Now, Frank's relationship to Brian and the church could have been used as a scapegoat why they didn't report it to the law about the time they sacked him! I believe with all my heart that the reason for not reporting Frank at that time is a thing called fame and money. Hillsong racks in millions every year and they didn't want the boat to be rocked. (May be it was that cart again, you know the one that the church of the day used to try and bring in God's presence the wrong way as Hillsong is doing now and it cost them). I strongly believe Brian's love for fame and money far out weighed his love for his father, so he threw him to the wolves at the Royal Commission, making out that he and the church are so righteous, that Frank and his acts of child abuse were so 'repulsive'. Doesn't it say somewhere in the bible that the love of money is the root of all evil? Maybe you have read this also, and as we read through the books of Kings and Chronicles of the Old Testament you start to see that some religious kings or leaders of that day had no hesitation about killing off there own relatives or others, for that matter, when they perceived or thought they perceived their bottom line was threatened. Oh, how money, power and prestige does some terrible things to some people! Gee, again it sounds like the religious leaders that sold out our lord to the Romans so they would get rid of him and out of the way, thus stopping him affecting their bottom line as well! While we are on the subject, it is said that some people want Brian and possibly Hillsong brought to account for not reporting Frank to the law. They had approximately fourteen years before the Royal Commission was started and I believe they knew long before that what frankie boy was up to! Now that the royal commission has confirmed what I have written, I hope this will show the church this type of misconduct needs to be dealt with at its conception.

In the bible it talks about a self-righteous, rich young ruler, who had come to Jesus and asked how he could get saved, Mark 10:17-27. I believe that this young man was being a little bit sarcastic when he fell on his knees and called Jesus 'good teacher' (I believe he said this in a sarcastic flattering way) and 'what must I do to inherit eternal life?' Jesus saw through this and called him to account. This person was misled or was fooling himself that his past life was righteous before God. This is why he fell on his knees and said what he did because he thought that Jesus couldn't offer him anything more to inherit eternal life and did it in a sarcastic way, testing Jesus! Jesus said that there was only one that was good and that was God. The Lord could see this was a works orientated righteousness in this young man. (He was rich, had prestige by being a ruler, possibly in the synagogue and did good things and must have thought he had it all together). Jesus went on to show where he missed the mark and asked him about keeping the 10 commandments and went on to bring some of them out. Do not murder, do not commit adultery, do not steal etc, etc, but, I believe Jesus deliberately didn't ask about keeping the first commandment which is 'you shall have no other gods (idols) before me', Exodus 20:3. The young ruler replied that he had done this from his youth up! Jesus in verse 21 felt a love for him and wanted him to come to repentance by bring out his lack, so he asked him to sell all he had and give to the poor that he may have treasures in heaven and follow him. The very fact was he had not kept the commandments at all, and he had an idol that he put before God, and broke the first commandment, and if you break one commandment you break the lot, that idol was his riches! Jesus went on to prove his point by saying that keeping the commandments to the letter was impossible and there was only one way to inherit eternal life and he had to repent, make Jesus Lord (because he was indeed God) and follow him. The words Jesus said to him flattened the young self righteous man and he could see his fault but wouldn't put into practise what Jesus asked him to do because he had great wealth and it was still his God! Some versions of this account of this rich young man say he was very sincere when he fell on his knees before the Lord and truly wanted salvation, I don't believe it at all, because he didn't repent after the greatest person on earth got to the truth of the matter! A very good friend of mine indicated that Jesus loved the young man, and rightly said! Jesus called a spade a spade as he did when he pulled Peter up and called him satan, as found in Matthew 16:23. Jesus still loved Peter but had to correct him and he didn't mince words doing it! Mark 4:19 warns us about the deceitfulness of riches. the rich young ruler was deluded as I believe are so many churches today! They are relying on their riches to build the kingdom of God and riches have become an IDOL that has got them by the short and curly. It is causing so many to miss the mark and by the way, Jesus has designed the way he wants His church built!

God will not be mocked by this type of thing and I stronly believe christians need to wake up to what is going on in much of the church and separate themselves from it as the word declares. God has so much more for you than to get caught up in the garbage that so many of these money hungry, Babylon, glits and glamour type churches are up to. The love of money does lead churches to do evil, so run, get out of them as fast as you can, go like the clappers and ask God to lead you to a true gathering of his people. You will find you will come into such a freedom and ask yourself why you didn't do it years ago! The lord will guide you as He did when, through the prophet Isaiah, foretold to the people of the Southern kingdom of Israel (Judah) what to do when they were in captivity; Isaiah 48:20 (niv) "leave Babylon, flee from the Babylonians"! he also foretold that God would look after them in verse 21 as He did when He brought the people out of Egypt. "They did not thirst when He led them through the desert; He made water flow for them from the rock (Jesus the rock); He split the rock and water gushed. Verse 22 "there is no peace for the wicked" says the Lord. In your spirit, I believe God is preparing you to come out, you know something is not quite right where you are attending, not quite kosher! Isaiah 52:12 "but you will not leave in haste or in flight; for the Lord will go before you, "He will prepare the way for you" but we must take that faith step, as Abraham did when God called him out of his country, but didn't know where he was going. In Genesis 12:1 "and the God of Israel will be your rear guard.

This is a song sung by Boney M that goes something like this: "let the words of our mouth and the meditation of our heart be acceptable in thy sight here tonight - by the rivers of Babylon, there we sat down, there we wept, when we remembered Zion (high place in God, where God really dwells) - now how shall we sing the Lords songs in a strange land". I believe this is a word from the Lord! How can we bring true worship while we are in these Babylon type churches, with their riches and arrogance? Not only in these type of churches but ministry on TV or even coming to our cities with false gospels! Check it out for yourself to see if it is so.

# 18

# Be On Guard and Let Jesus Rule

The sin of association is something that we all have to be wary of; let me try to explain! There was a king in the Old Testament named Jehoshaphat who allied with bad guys, other kings of Israel, the first one was King Ahab. In those days the nation of Israel was divided into two kingdoms and often they would war against each other. King Jehoshaphat had fortified his cities against this type of thing, but must have presumed there was a better way of protecting his assets by marriage into the other king's family 2 Chronicles 18:1. Jehoshaphat did have a real love for the Lord, but like the rest of us had weaknesses and his coming together with Ahab nearly cost him his life! King Ahab wasn't just a bad guy; he was very wicked in the eyes of the Lord. 1 Kings 16:30-33 (NIV) Ahab had married a woman named Jezebel, who was not a Jew and worshiped other gods. Jezebel was a pagan princess and was the daughter of Ethbaal, King of Sidon or Phoenicia. The main god that she worshiped was Baal, a god of ancient Canaan and Phoenicia. Baal means lord and was the god of fertility, of helping the earth to produce crops and humans to produce offspring, it was also said to control the rain. (Elijah proved that wrong).

Baal was worshiped in the form of a bull symbolising strength and fertility, but often there was a human sacrifice involved, usually the first born of the one making the sacrifice and was made to appease Baal when things didn't seem to be working out too well. It seems that Baal features later on in the Roman and Greek cultures as well. Both these cultures were very much like many churches and so called leaders in God's church today. Never satisfied, always after more money, legalistic, controlling, keeping the people that are caught up in their deception busy, busy, busy so as never coming to truth that would set them free, sacrificing the truth of God to build there own empire. When Israel came out of Egypt and Moses went up Mount Sinai to speak with the Lord, the people got impatient that Moses had been away so long and corrupted them-selves by allowing Aaron to make a golden calf idol and many turned away from Yahweh, their true God, Exodus 32:1-29.(NIV) By turning away from God and worshiping other gods, the people quickly started to indulge in revelry, worshiping the god's of the flesh and it turned into nothing more than a sex orgy! These were a people that God had saved out of their bondage, did great things which they could see only the true God could do! And yet when the man of God, whom God used to bring them out of Egypt, left them for awhile, they turned back to the way of the world. Baal worship is very much in the church today, grandeur, rich is right, false doctrine, prosperity teaching and word of faith movements. Satan has run amok in some areas of the church and I believe that our Lord is rising up a people and through them will stand up against this rubbish. The church has been sold a load of cow's dung (sorry, dung makes things grow); much of the stuff handed out by these false teachers will kill you! So let's get on our knees and ask the Lord of Host to reveal truth that will set us free; let us get to a place where nothing else matters except him, Jesus, the Lord of Lord and the King of Kings, the risen Lord, once again making him Lord and King of our lives and of the church.

After King Ahab was killed in battle that both kings were involved in, King Jehoshaphat was coming back to the safety of his palace in Jerusalem, a prophet by the name of Jehu came up to him and said "Should you help the wicked and love those who hate the Lord?" 2 Chronicles: 19:1-3.(NIV) A very big rebuke from the Lord! Ahaziah, King Ahab's son became king after Ahab was killed in the battle. Now, I don't think that King Jehoshaphat went to the school of the prophets (mind you it wasn't around in those days, but it did come in a bit later); I think he must have gone to the school of slow learners, and as I look back over the years I must have gone to the same school! Jehoshaphat made an alliance with the new king of Israel, Ahaziah, who was guilty of wickedness before the Lord, 2 Chronicles 20:35-37 (NIV) and between them they constructed a fleet of trading ships, but God destroyed them. Again, a prophet named Eliezer prophesied against Jehoshaphat for aligning himself with the wrong people. Wow, heavy stuff, we need to take note of for our own leaning and safety! Not to associate or get involved with such people but sometimes we don't see it right away and it can take a working of the Holy Spirit to open our spiritual eyes to see this.

Paul, the apostle, wrote to his offsider Timothy in 2 Timothy 3:1-7 (NIV) "But mark this: there will be terrible times in the last days! People will be lovers of themselves; lovers of money, boastful, proud, abusive, disobedient to their parents, ungrateful, unholy, without love, unforgiving, slanderous, without self-control, brutal, not lovers of the good, treacherous, rash, conceited, lovers of pleasure rather than lovers of God, having a form of Godliness but denying its power (to change the heart). These are so called Christians he's talking about. Verse 6 "Have nothing to do with them; they are the kind who worm their way into homes and gain control over weak willed women". Let's go to what Jesus says about the spirit of the Pharisees in Matthew 23:14(KJV) (some Bible versions didn't put this in, but I believe it's of God because Paul confirms it as truth) "Woe to you, Scribes and Pharisees, hypocrites! For you devour widows' houses and for pretence you make long prayers, (trying to make out how holy and righteous they are) therefore you will receive the greater condemnation". I am convinced that its not just weak willed woman that so much of this is happening to but men in the church as well, through Christian TV and other mediums. I was talking to a female friend not too long ago. This friend, who doesn't have a lot, told me that she used to give to one of these overpowering television preachers. It sounded like it was a fair bit of money over time! She was a woman who because of the situation that she had come out of and being only a new born again Christian, she was drawn into this type of ministry. God got her out of it because of her love for Him. This lady is not a weak willed woman, but a person that is growing in him, learning to hear from God to know the difference between false and truth. It's something we all need to come into! I'm afraid that many, so called preachers of Jesus Christ, church leaders have been caught up in this nonsense that these false ministers have brought to the church! She said she didn't feel right in her spirit about what she was doing and the Lord showed her that the only people making money or been blessed by her giving was the false TV ministry. She turned around and put the junk the ministry had sent her on a garbage truck and sent it to the rubbish tip where their teaching belonged! She told me she came into a real peace and liberty that only the true God can give. This was Kenneth Copeland Ministries that she had been giving to! Copeland is someone who was on the internet gloating and boasting that his ministry had past the billion dollar mark, sent in by, I believe, gullible and deceived people of God. God told him (which God he talking about I wonder, that money Jesus again) not to think in millions but billions. I also believe this man on TV said Jesus wore designer suits or clothes, laughing and trying to justify his over the top expensive suit he wears! Yes, Jesus did wear a seamless garment (which would have been quite expensive in those days) when he went to the cross. It was symbolic of the high priest who wore a seamless garment, taking the blood of animals into the Holy of Holies to sprinkle over the Ark of the Covenant and there about for his sins and the sins of the people, which had to be repeated every year. Jesus Christ is our great high priest taking his own blood before the presence of the most high God for all the sins of the world, but only once for ever and ever! How could false minister Copeland even think that Jesus wore a seamless garment to justify the over the top expensive suits he wears! How deceived and sick can you get? Money, greed and fame have so blinded him and many like him to such a degree that it so wrong, and yet there are so many people with itching ears following these jokers, how sad! Jesus warns us about the deceitfulness of riches; Matthew 13:22 and Mark 4:19 which can take us away from truth. These jokers boast and gloat how much money they bring in and what they are doing for the Lord's work. (Which Lord are they talking about?) How far have we, the church of Jesus Christ gone away from truth by letting these jokers hoodwink us? Remember, "The greedy will not inherit the kingdom of God", 1 Corinthians 6:10.

It reminds me of when King David counted the people of Israel, which he wasn't allowed to under their law. God allowed it to happen to show what was in David's heart, and not only David's but the people as well! God used Satan to incite the king to take this census, 1 Chronicles 21:1. The people belonged to the Lord and King David wasn't to look to them for his strength to overcome his enemies or to achieve any work for the Lord, but he was to continually look to God as the one that was his helper and provider. Pride had come into David's heart, thinking of what possibly had been achieved through his ministry and big noting himself, but all it did was to show David and the people what was in their hearts. Pride and arrogance had come into the folk that were involved in David's ministry as well; just like many of the churches today, big and rich, thinking they have done so much for God and because of that have gone away from their first love. God punished David and the people by using a plague to kill off 70,000 men, 2 Samuel 24:10-17, men in this case speaks of the strength of the flesh and leadership. 70,000 speak of complication and perfection; anything with the number 7 always speaks of these things.  God killed off that which had led the then church into a wrong way of thinking and was bringing them back to the right way of thinking!  This is something we must take note of; David was not only the one that God dealt with but many of the people as well because they had got caught up in his sin and it revealed their hearts.

# 19

# Responsibility of Leaders

Leaders have a great responsibility in how they lead the people and we must keep praying for them. We all can make mistakes, as was the case in David's life, but the thing I love about David and I have said this before, was that when pointed out his faults he repented right away. He had a true heart after the Lord. God is not against big churches or money but watch out when these things start to take control of us, becoming the gods we worship and arrogance and pride rise up in the leaders and the people as well! When I think of the so called false leaders in the church today; oh where is the true gospel of Jesus Christ with this lot of money hungry wolves that come to devour God's flock and fleece them? These types of preachers are nothing more than snake oil salesmen selling a false gospel used to line their own pockets and ego! When you hear them preach, its sounds like they know what they are talking about; they preach Jesus and it sounds like they are drawing people to him and teaching people the way of salvation, but, and I mean but, it's drawing people to themselves and exploiting money out of them, all in the name of the gospel. God is longing for a father-child relationship and this is what he wants all of us to come into. Jesus has placed leaders and ministry in the church to help bring this about, but instead of, as in many cases, the hierarchy have used their gifts and calling to build up themselves at the expense of the people!

The bible tells us quite clearly not to use the gospel to build wealth, their agendas are so wrong and I believe these people are driven by a wrong spirit that controls and manipulates them, but they can't see it. We have the same type of ministry in Australia, trying to sell a load of crock to Christians that don't know God well enough. I went to a church a while ago to hear a so called preacher speak. His name was Pat Mesiti from the eastern states. As far as I could make out he is a pastor and has something to do with Hillsong church in Sydney, boy oh boy that doesn't surprise me one little bit! Hillsong is a church, that was started or helped start by a man who had a lot of input the way it was to be run, had been accused of perverted sin in the seventies, refused to receive correction until it was brought out in the nineties and he had to confess it because of the evidence against him. All those years he carried on in that sin, leading a church and organisation without repentance, so as far as I believe the church, Hillsong, was started by a wrong foundation and a wrong spirit. Hillsong is known by its music! They use this to get crowds in, then as the people are amusingly stirred they hit them with giving, preying on the people's senses. Music and money have become the gods to many churches and Hillsong would have to be tops. Money and music are the golden calves to that church! No wonder the leaders of Hillsong, like Frank Houston, teach tithing like a law, money mad with all the Hollywood style of outward appearance of being holy but all its doing is glorifying the flesh and worshiping other gods, also making a few rich! Folks, God will not be mocked. Hillsong seems more like a cult, the blind leading the blind, more and more people worshiping the church and the music that they produce. A TV reporter in an interview with a young person at a Hillsong meeting asked why the person came along and they replied "To hear the music!". I believe Hillsong uses music to attract people more to them than it's designed to worship and please God, it is nothing more than a worldly enterprise as it was in the days of Jesus when he drove the wicked, false worshipers out of his Father's house. They use the name of Jesus to justify what they are doing, but I believe he was never invited in, how could have he been if the foundations were laid wrong! Don't be fooled by crowds, Adolf Hitler and the Dalai Lama draw big crowds as well and there is nothing holy about them! These men might seem to be miles apart in their work and life, and their doctrines are so far off, yet so many people seemed to think what they have said or say is so correct. In the end their doctrines will benefit no one. Unless Jesus is Lord of all then he's not Lord at all and he was not or is Lord of those two men, yet crowds have flocked to see and hear them.

    I had heard the name Pat Mesiti, somewhere before but couldn't remember where! He is no more than a high power salesman selling his motivation tapes through the gospel of Jesus Christ. He used misrepresented scripture to try and get us to believe that all Christians should be rich and one could use his method to achieve this goal, nothing about asking God if it's his will! One of the things he did was he asked the people to put up their hands to show who wanted to become millionaires, and many did. I and others were sickened by the overall performance he put on in God's house of worship that day. He finished this sham with a deliberate lie by saying that those that wanted his product he could let it go at lower price, but only on that day. He owns the business so really if he wanted to drop the price he could do it on any day! This is one of the great con tricks used by salespeople and it's nothing new. I was looking around to see if Jesus was there to drive him out with a whip as he did when he drove all the other con artists out of his Father's house! To me it just shows how immature the leaders of that church, Kingdom City, Wangara, Perth, that the sham was performed in and I don't believe anything has changed! They need a good kick in their butt for not checking out this joker first! To feed rubbish like that to God's people is ridiculous but in understanding that church a little better now, I have come to realise that the ministry of that church have little more than a head knowledge of God, strong willed, charismatic, with very young leaders and others as well, who have very little experience of being in the world as Jesus did. They haven't developed a true maturity or understanding of what the people in churches go through, and I feel this is what Paul was doing when he set up leadership in his churches! He was indicating that leaders needed an understanding of family in the natural, been through it and uses this as a bench mark on how the churches should be run, with a true fathers heart. So many churches, as I believe Kingdom City is, are more interested in building more monuments to them; it's more of a numbers game, and how much money they can con out of the people they have been entrusted with, than feeding the flock the best of the anointed word with a true father's heart. This type of ministry is going on in so many churches today! Maybe they did look into Mesiti's ministry first and agreed this type of thing is acceptable in God's house. I believe this is how far we have fallen in Christendom today, deceived and being deceived. I went out into the foyer after the service to confront Mesiti but he was surrounded by a lot of people wanting buy his stuff and I felt it wasn't expedient to do it at that time! Really, if this is what leaders allow to minister in their churches, and is acceptable to them, it shows how very little they understand what God's true church is all about. They don't understand that the Lord wants true worship, in spirit and truth, which can only be done through the working of the Holy Spirit's leading and not by the spirit of man. The church has become more of an entertainment centre, a circus, than a true place of worship unto our Lord! I heard a very well known preacher not too long ago on You-tube, a man that was very upset the way the church over all has gone. This preachers name was David Wilkinson from the USA, a man that has been used mightily by God, but a few years back was taken in a car accident! Wilkinson said in one of his messages, that many churches through the US have been started by young men, intelligent, strong willed, gifted etc, they get the crowds, preach up a storm and leave a trail of destruction and disillusionment. I believe that this type of thing is not only in US but Australia and possibly the rest of the West as well. I believe many of these youngsters don't have a clue what the Lord is wanting in His church. God is looking for the father's heart to be manifested from the leaders to the people, as the first apostles did; Paul is a great example of this! Oh church let us get back to the true gospel of what God is wanting and not what we want! Money, money, money, build, build, build, huff puff and bulldust! No wonder people fall away! No wonder the world thinks we are no better than them. I believe this is why so many Christians are dissatisfied with what is going on in many churches today! But I also believe that the Lord is putting the axe to the root of the problem and is bring back truth, to bring in once more His Glory and not mans.

# 20

# Let's Get Away From the Pig Pens

When the Prodigal son In Luke 15:11-32 left his father's house, he took with him his goods and money, the bible says he went into a far away country and got involved in loose living, which chewed up all his assets. Because he was broke and desperate he then got a job looking after someone's pigs, which to a Jew is an abomination because their law states that pigs are unclean, not to be eaten or even touched. The son was starving and came to his senses, then headed home, knowing back there he was far better off. The father saw him at a distance heading home and because of his great love for this lost son, ran to embrace and greet him, welcoming him back with open arms that only a true father could give. Today in many cases God's people don't have to go to a far country to get involved in the rubbish of the pig pen because so much of it has come into the church! Oh, where is the gospel of repentance that Peter preached on the day of Pentecost! Where oh where is the gospel of taking up your cross and following the Lord daily, denying ourselves of things that would take us away from true fellowship with our true God and not with the gods of the flesh! What these false gospel preachers are doing is glorifying the flesh, drawing attention to them and to their ministry by letting us know how big some of their churches are and how much money they rake in, how many people come along to hear their deceived rubbish that flows out of their mouth and others like them. It's not glorifying the Lord, only themselves and they don't have any qualms about boasting about it either.

It makes me feel sick with the falseness of these people, with all their glamour and Hollywood-style way of doing things. These are people with charismatic personalities, strong willed people that are strong in the flesh and are leading the church to some degree down the gurgler! They gather around them 'yes people', people that don't know God very well either! Sending half trained people out so they can make a name for themselves by starting other churches. These are false leaders not looking after the flock they have been entrusted with; how can they when they are tearing around all over the place taking their rubbish message with them and training others how to be as bad as themselves? These people don't have a true father's heart, and if you don't agree with them, or they feel threatened by you or others, their reactions can be like the pit of hell itself spewed out against you. These so called leaders are never content, always after more money to build more and more monuments to themselves! Always prepared to suck more money out of the flock to do it, all in the name of the Lord! When you think of the first Christians, who didn't have very much substance to work with, using only their faith and a complete dedication to the Lord, they turned the world upside down. These folk were looking forward to their reward in heaven; they were looking forward to something far better than what they could get down here.

Praise God, praise God that the true, born again believers are starting to question what's going on in Christendom today. I strongly believe that the Lord God is saying to the church today to come out from amongst them and be separate, from false prophets, false teachers, people that would lead the church away from the true anointed word, the word that will set us free and bring us into a greater relationship with our God! There are many false prophets, teachers and even apostles in the world today, many of them are in Christian churches, on Christian TV and some even travelling round the world in their luxury jet planes. Some times someone sends me stuff on You-tube and I do allow myself to watch some of it! Sometimes it is good old fashioned preachers coming against false preachers, and sometimes its false preachers themselves bring in their false rubbish. One of the best ways of stopping their ministry is by not giving money to them; starve them of what their lust craves for. These people don't have a father's heart for the people they minister to, how could they? They are more interested in the money they can fleece out of you. I know, I was stupid and got sucked out of money by one of Oral Roberts' deceived systems many years ago. At his university site he's got a statue of praying hands, (how religious can you get) praying alright, preying money out of gullible Christians; I believe this ministry is only one of many that the Lord is exposing from the rooftops today!

# 21

# Let's Get Back To Rightly Dividing the Word

I try not to watch too much stuff on Christian TV, which I don't have anyway, or stuff on You-tube. I try to get into God's word, which brings me into a greater understanding of Jesus and his ways! I do at times Google different ministries to get their point of view on things and weigh it up with God's word. I watched a segment by David Wilkerson exposing the false prophet Benny Hinn. A man that said God would destroy the homosexual community sometime in the mid-nineties, hey did it happen? (A false prophet, under the Old Testament would have been killed if what they prophesied didn't happen), Deuteronomy 18:20-22. I reckon that community has got bigger and why? Because so much of the truth of God's anointing has lifted off the church which has been hoodwinked by these false men and woman that many Christians think are of God! Which God are they of? Oh church let use get back to our first love with our saviour and Lord. Any person that brings down curses on people and their children on TV because they don't agree with their ministry as Hinn did and possibly still does, a man that said he wishes he had a Holy Ghost machine gun so he can wipe out folk that come against his ministry; you can see it all on You-tube and make up your own mind. Where oh where is the grace and love of God in that type of ministry? Gee this sounds so much like the chief priests and Pharisees in John 7:46, when they said the people were accursed because they were starting to believe in Jesus and they didn't know the scriptures or the law as well as them! When you think of a man like Benny Hinn being so upset, as he is about some people not agreeing with his ministry, you have to ask yourself; in what spirit does he operates? Again I say it sounds like the chief priests and Pharisees! Is it the truth that these folks say about Hinn's ministry and others like him that upsets these jokers? Yes I believe it is.

The bible says "by their fruit we shall know them". Is it because they feel threatened by these upstarts that speak against these impostors of the true gospel of Jesus Christ? Yes I believe it is! Just like Saul when the Lord left him and then sent an evil spirit forcefully upon him, what was in his heart manifested itself against God's chosen king, David! Saul felt jealousy and anger against David to such a degree that he wanted him out of the way, in other words dead, 1 Samuel 18:8-11. When you read verse 10 it states "The next day an evil spirit from the Lord came forcefully upon Saul. He was prophesying in his house, while David was playing his harp, as he usually did." Two different things were happening here, David was worshiping God in his playing of the harp, but Saul was acting like an uncontrolled loony!

As far as I can make out, the Hebrew to explain this word prophesying, in this situation in which Saul was involved in, was uncontrolled ecstatic behaviour. Paul said in the church let everything be done decently and in order; he also said to make sure this happens because if the situation gets out of hand, people off the street could come in and say this is nothing more than a nut house. (I'm using poetic license here). He also said that we are to have a sound mind and the Spirit of the prophet was subject to the prophet. In other words it was up to us to make sure that everything was done decently and in order. Boy, I have seen some nutty things done in the church over the years! All in the name of the Lord, yeah sure it was. No one can tell me many of Hinn's shows are nothing more that. I personally don't believe that it's the Holy Spirit that's causing the people that have gone along to watch his show, to perform like they do when he waves his coat or his hand around or even when he kicks his foot in the air and people fall backwards. I noticed in one show that he had some 'yes men' up on the stage with him and he said that Jesus was standing on one part of it with them. He pointed out to them where He was and told them to approach Him but they would not be able to keep standing before Him. One by one the 'yes men' approached the spot and like humpty dumpty they all fell down. I noticed they didn't fall on areas that would hurt them or each other. Nevertheless, I believe its going to take all the king's horses and all the king's men to fix up the deceived mess parts of the church have got itself into by allowing themselves to get caught up with this type of nonsense!! Another time Benny was making out the Holy Spirit was so heavily upon him and he put on a great act that he couldn't stand and every time he wanted to get up he couldn't, the poor deluded Christians at his show and I guess watching on TV thought it was from the Lord, oh which one I wonder? It's nothing more than mass hysteria nonsense governed by a wrong spirit, glorifying the flesh, Hinn and others like him elevating themselves as someone great in the eyes of God. Then the showman come out with a great big unholy ghost vacuum cleaner and sucks all the money out of the poor unrepenting people. Again I am using poetic license. These types of preachers have a very controlling spirit on them (the spirit of Jezebel) and can make you feel condemned if you don't give and tell you God won't bless you unless you do, indicating the more you give the bigger the blessing (for them). The good news is that Jesus didn't come to condemn but brought liberty and freedom and if you feel condemned by these false preachers, for goodness sake don't give. Preachers who wear funny looking suits, (as Hinn does) white suits, flashy suits or outfits to draw attention to themselves and its nothing more than glorifying the flesh. They will stand and say what they are doing for the Lord and I hear the Lord replying, GET AWAY FROM ME I NEVER KNEW YOU! This nonsense that these jokers put on, to me, is no more than an entertainment circus for the crowds to be drawn into but God will not be mocked. Their Hollywood style of doing things, flashy suits, hair style, flashing lights, smoke etc (many churches use this type of thing as well) to give some sort of effect that this is what Christianity is all about, it's no more than pandering to the flesh, as Hollywood does, and not to the crucified Christ that brings people to true repentance!

What is so tragic about this type of ministry is as Paul said that many of these people can start off with the right spirit (Holy Spirit) and God has given them gifts and callings "without repentance", Romans 11:29 but go off the rails because they take the glory to self and I believe a wrong spirit takes over!! Paul again writing to Timothy in 1 Timothy 6:6-11 "but godliness with contentment is great gain. We brought nothing into the world, and we can take nothing out of it. But if we have food and clothing, we will be content with that". People who want to get rich fall into temptation and a trap and into many foolish and harmful desires that plunge men into ruin and destruction. "For the love of money is the root of all kinds of evil. Some people, eager for money, have wandered from the faith and pierced themselves with many griefs. But you man of God, flee from all of this and pursue righteousness, godliness, faith, love, endurance and gentleness." Paul was warning Timothy not to get caught up in the money thing that has got hold of so many so called church leaders to day! People who want to build mega churches, as well as people on TV who always seem to be asking for more and more money to make a name for themselves, to live an over the top life style and tell us that it was God that provided; what out and out utter bull. Years ago when some of these jokers were on free TV, and possibly still are today, I used to watch some of them and I remember at times being put off because of the glitz and glamour on how these ministries were set up. Why would anybody want to bring Christ to others like Hollywood? Which is hell bent on destroying anything good and holy that the gospel brings. They don't give stuff about anything except money and it seems they don't care how they get it! There is so much undermining violence and smut going on in movies and entertainment today; that there is very few that you can watch. (I like movies, but you have to be careful). Satan has control of that Hollywood mob, but they can't see it or they don't want to see it and many preachers in the church are in the same boat, rowing in the wrong direction, deceiving and being deceived! Jude 1:11-13 puts it this way; "Woe to them that have taken the way of Cain (killing off any thing that is righteousness before God), they have rushed for profit into the error of Balaam, (people that are more interested in profit and motivated by greed than doing God's will), they have been destroyed in Korah's rebellion, verse 12 (people that want to be up front, without any real understanding of God's word) these men are blemishes at your love feast, eating with you without the slightest qualm; shepherds who feed only themselves. They are clouds without rain, blown along by the wind; autumn trees without fruit and uprooted-twice dead. They are wild waves of the sea, foaming up their shame; wandering stars, for whom blackest darkness has been reserved for ever". Jeremiah 5:26-31 lets us know that we have these people among us but sadly many people love it so, verse 26 "Among my people are wicked men who lie in wait like men that snare birds and like those that set traps that catch men. Like cages full of birds, their houses are full of deceit; they have become rich and powerful and have grown fat (rich) and sleek (cunning). Their evil deeds have no limits; they do not plead the case of the fathers to win it, they do not defend the rights of the poor. Should I not punish them for this?" declares the Lord. "Should I not avenge myself on such a nation (ministry) as this? A horrible and shocking thing has happened in the land: (church) the prophets prophesy lies; the priests rule by their own authority, (not hearing from God, but in their own flesh) and my people love it this way. But what will you do in the end?"

It has been reported that the City Harvest Church in Singapore, a mega church which draws in huge crowds! Six of their leaders on 20th October 2015 have been found guilty of misappropriating, as far as I can make out, $50 million of the church funds and falsifying the churches accounts to cover up their misdeeds. The founder, Kong Hee, is one of those found guilty! It sounds like the City News which is linked to the church tried to water down the situation. Gee that sound like another church that tried to water down a situation they got themselves into as well. When my son told me about what was happening to City Harvest Church, I got into the internet to find out more, it upset me no end and I thought "I hope they throw the book at them and throw away the key". When we turn to the letter of 1 John (NIV) he goes on to exclaim 1 John: 9-10 "Anyone who claims to be in the light but hates a brother or sister is still in darkness. Verse 10 Anyone who loves their brother and sister lives in the light, and there is nothing in them to make them stumble (make who stumble? his brothers and sisters), verse 11 but anyone who hates his brother or sister is in the darkness and walks around in darkness. They do not know where they are going, because the darkness has blinded them". These are strong words but what John is saying, if we really love our brother and sister we will do everything possible not to make our brother and sisters stumble. You can't tell me the situation which has gone on in City Harvest church hasn't made many stumble. Since 2010, as it is in print, about a quarter of the church people have left and that was before the verdict was brought down by the court. Christian people that have put there hope in these false people will, in many cases, be devastated, shattered. People will say that Satan is attacking the church, and God may well be using him to rock the boat (cart). But I truly believe that God is saying, "Get the church back the way I want it and not the way man wants it." It doesn't mean that we want to fail at times, but if we do, our relationship with God will make us quickly repent and get it right (as King David did). Just think for a moment about the leader of that mega church, Kong Hee, getting up and telling the congregation how much he loved them and fleecing the flock to pay for his wife's singing career at the same time. Did he love his brothers and sisters? Not according to the bible! Kong Hee has been sentenced to eight years in prison for his part in this charade! I pray that his time spent inside, as it was with Jimmy Baker, who was sentenced to five years after he was caught with his hand in the till, will also come to a place of repentance. I believe God is exposing this type of thing because he loves us and it's not his will that any should go to hell. This crime that these six leaders had got into was going on for some time, and it makes you wonder if, as in churches like Hillsong, City Harvest Church and so many others that are in the same boat, are really born again type Churches? What do I mean by born again type churches?

In Matthew 28:18-19 Jesus told his disciples to make disciples of all nations into His name and to teach them to obey everything He commanded them. It seems that many churches around the world, because of the moving of God, do produce many born again babies, but as I have pointed out in this book, many churches don't' bring their kids up with a true fathers heart. Brian Houston from Hillsong Church Sydney, not that long ago in an interview said something like this. "That he was going to go back to his church and become a father to them!" What? After all these years running the show he was now going to become a father to his church. True fathers start at been a father from year dot and Hillsong Church has been going since about 1983. Why now? Was it because the Royal Commission was getting too close to the matter about him and the church not reporting his father's sex sins to the police fourteen years back and people would like to see justice served. I have written right through this book about true fathers of the church and money mad ministries. I really believe with all my heart they don't mix, read about the first apostles and especially Paul. Again, those other ministries are more like a Saulish type ministry, controlling, legalistic, dogmatic, money hungry, etc, fleecing the flock to fulfill their lusts, not true fathers at all

They are not bringing up their kids according to the pattern that Jesus laid down in his word, with the leading and guidance of the Holy Spirit. The Gospel is more than being born again, that's only the start, it's about truly growing in Jesus, by the help of true fathers and mothers who go out of their way to bring them up to know God according to the full Gospel, in spirit and in truth. These charlatans get the people in, and then use them as a commodity to use up, without ever loving them as you would a new born baby. These false leaders don't live in the light of the gospel, but are blinded by their own lusts, living in complete darkness as the word declares. These are not true shepherds at all, not laying down their lives for the flock but using them up for their own ends. Proverbs 16:8 (NIV) states "Better a little with righteousness than much gain with injustice". Know wonder people are falling away because there are leaders like this in the churches and on TV. I believe it's so much to do with the way they wrongly perceive the way the gospel is operated! So much of this rubbish, in one way or another is going on in the church of Jesus Christ today, and I believe much of it is related to the prosperity gospel and its false teachings. I hate repeating myself, but if you live by the flesh, which Satan (the serpent) has every right to feed on, it will kill you. Satan (the serpent) eats the dust of the earth with which we are made from and if we live by the flesh he will eat us up, spit out the bones, expose us to the world and we will die spiritually! Genesis 3:14. (NIV) In the book of Revelation 3:14-22, if there is one church that revivals what many churches and ministries are up to today it would be the Church of Laodicea! Rich, does not need a thing, but in Gods eyes is wretched, pitiful, blind and naked. Jesus counseled them to get back to the way He builds His church. To bring in the gold (attitudes, trials, right teaching) that is refined through the fire and not by fleecing the flock, which is carried out by so many ministries. To cover their nakedness and put on clean white clothes, thus showing true repentance from their god of riches, which reflect what is really going on in the heart. To allow God to heal their eyes to see truth again, this will bring them to a relationship what Jesus is looking for in His church, getting back to His way of doing things!

Oh church of Jesus Christ, ask God to reveal what is going on in much of the church today, draw closer to him and he will draw .When Paul wrote to the Corinthian church, one of the things he was trying to do was to correct them because false apostles had come in and tried to undermine his work. They told the people that Paul was not a real apostle at all and they shouldn't take any notice of him; they were deceiving the people that they were the true apostles and the people were to do what they said and not what Paul said. Through the letters Paul brought out where these jokers missed the mark in God. One of the things he brought out in 2 Corinthians 2:17 (NIV) "Unlike so many, we do not peddle the word of God for profit. On the contrary, in Christ we speak before God with sincerity like men sent from God". Paul didn't charge money when he preached the gospel to them, unlike so many that were using the gospel to feather their own nests. Things haven't changed over the years, same old, same old. As it was then so it is very much like it today, maybe even worse!! These false people are like the prophets of Baal in 1 Kings 18:25-30 (NIV) when Elijah challenged them to build an altar and the people to help him build one as well to put a sacrifice on to see which God would consume it by fire thus showing every one, the people (Christians if you like) and the false prophets of Baal who the true God was! The false prophets tried first and there was a lot of show, noise, and dancing around the altar trying to get the attention of their god, but no response. Elijah, then started to mock them by asking if their god had gone away or was having a nap? Verse 28 states that they shouted louder and slashed themselves with swords and spears, as was their custom until their blood flowed. Isn't this so much like these showy type ministries today who use entertainment to get the crowd in and put on a superficial act by asking them to make a decision for Jesus. There are in many cases, in my opinion, no real repentance, no real commitment to the Lord, just little bits of cuts and a bit of blood, all outward appearance of coming to the Lord, but not making him Lord! My God uses his word which is alive and active, sharper than a two edged sword, dividing soul and spirit, cutting through the bone and marrow, judging the thoughts and attitudes, getting to the heart of sin which brings true repentance, making Jesus Lord, not this outward garbage that we see in many churches and on TV today, Hebrew 4:12 (NIV). So many people that make a decision to the Lord, I believe don't make a heart decision at all but only of the mind and that only for a short time, not a true commitment to follow Jesus. I love looking at the gospel of John 8:30-58. (NIV) Many Jews who Jesus was talking to, put their faith in him and Jesus knowing better tested them to see where they were at and found them wanting, they didn't really believe in him at all. By the time he had finished testing them, he told them that they didn't know the true God, verses 42-47, and the devil was their true father and after this situation they wanted to stone him, verse 58, thus showing what was really in their heart!

God is looking today for a people that are sold out to him and not to the golden calves of this world, a people who will not allow themselves to come under the influences of the false prophets that preach the way of the golden calf is the way to go. A people when they hear this type of message, will turn their backs to it, knowing it will hinder their relationship with the true God, Jesus! I believe that God is not mocked by these false worshipers and is bringing a people to true worship. I believe that God will unify his church, His true church, in these last days like we haven't seen before! When David overcame Goliath he did it because he knew his God! 1 Samuel 17:40 (NIV) "Then he (David) took his staff in his hand, which to me speaks of being lead by God, chose five smooth stones from the brook and put them in his shepherd's bag or wallet. His sling was his hand, and drew near the Philistine". The five stones speak to me of true shepherds, the five fold ministry gifts that God has put in the church, apostles, prophets, pastors, teachers and evangelists to help the church come to the place God wants it to come. Not just the people up front doing their stuff, but a people that are sold out to him! David got the stones out of the brook which to me is the word; water always speaks of the word of God. Smooth stones! People the word of God has worked on, through thick and thin, when the brook was running nicely and when it was a ragging torrent. A people that allowed God to mould them and shape them into what He want them for in these last days. David put the smooth stones into his shepherd's bag or wallet, a unity with Christ. Jesus Christ himself the Chief Shepherd, the Lord of all, with a people that are truly longing to see Him high and lifted up in the Church so as to draw all men to himself! A people prepared so he can use them to hit the mark when fired out of his sling to bring down the Goliaths of this world!

When the prophet Elijah came against the false prophets of Baal on Mt Carmel, God had prepared him by what he went through before this event happened. He had been obedient to the Lord, and the Lord kept him though the famine that ravished the lands. Elijah had got to know his God; he had built a relationship of not just knowing about God, but knowing God and that He is true to his word. Even though the odds were stacked against Elijah in the natural when he came against the false prophets, he didn't look to that but was looking to the Author and Finisher of his faith to win through. He had come to trust in God and not the situation or himself! Elijah was said by some to be a troublemaker in the church and some possibly said to him "Elijah, don't judge". People that don't know God well enough and His anointed word. Christians that are very carnal and try to work God out and His ways by their intellect, but its God that's building His church, not them! I pray that the Lord will rise up Christians today with the spirit of Elijah (trouble makers) who are sold out to God and I believe He is!

When you look into King Ahab's life and King Herod the greats life, you know the one that tried to kill Jesus when he was only a baby! We find they involved themselves in grandeur in building projects they had done. Again it sounds like so much of the church today. 1 Kings 22:39-40 speaks of Ahab inlaying his palace with ivory: gee, you would need a few elephants! No wonder there are none running around the top of Africa any more; he probably killed the lot. King Herod, before the time Jesus was born, had the Jewish temple enlarged to something quite huge and magnificent, far in excess of the original one that was repaired by people after they came out of captivity in Babylon. Also Solomon's temple before that, some call it Herod's temple. Mind you he imposed a tax to pay for it, gee that sounds like some churches! Both of these kings hated God, they hated His presence and tried to get rid of Him by killing off his representatives. In Ahab's case it was through his wife Jezebel and the prophets of the Lord, the ones that brought the true anointed word of the Lord to the church at that time and the same thing is happening in today's church because the spirit of Jezebel is very much alive in the church. Jezebel killed off many of God's prophets and replaced them with her own and because there are so many in the church today we, as Christians need to cry out to God for the gift of discernment to tell which are false and which are true. This is something we must work on constantly; as the spirit of Jezebel is so undermining, so cunning, that God's people who don't have a really strong relationship with our Lord can easily get swept up in it. I have said this before and I'll say it again, God is not looking for fair weather friends! The spirit of Jezebel at times will come across so religious and use scripture to justify what they do in the name of the Lord. The bible says in 1 Kings 21 there was a righteous man named Naboth who owned a vineyard which was his inheritance from his father. King Ahab, Jezebel's husband wanted it as a vegetable patch but Naboth wouldn't sell or exchange it to him because under their law he wasn't allowed to. Ahab went away and had a hissy fit. It states in verse 4 that he went home, lay down on his bed sulking and refused to eat. His wife, Jezebel found him like that and said she would get the vineyard for him. She did it by deceit and using the law to justify what she did, which ended with having Naboth stoned to death because of the trumped up charges brought against him by her using her husband's authority in Kings 8:14. This allowed Ahab to take possession of the vineyard he so desired. This illustration is type or shadow given to us to be aware of; we must rightly divide the word of God in humility, not just accepting everything because of the scripture involved. This is only one of many deceptions that the spirit of Jezebel will use in the church of Jesus Christ today.

Jezebel and the prophets of BAAL have stolen away from God's children much of the bread that produces life and have fed them rubbish that produces death. When we look back over the years and the stuff that has come into the church, stuff that glorifies the flesh, you know like, "You are the king's kids so you deserve the best and you should be prosperous and wealthy, confess these things and you will get them". Always building up our flesh and ego and not the character of Christ in us, always trying to get us to trust in the flesh and trying to get our minds off allowing the anointed word to work in us. Feeding our lusts for more and more of the same rubbish and nothing about the crucified life. The bible states that Jezebel and the prophets of Baal ate together at the same table in the palace, indicating they would have had the best of the food. When you think of all the money that has been poured into so called works of the Lord's projects, money used to build monuments to a man or organisation and all its doing is feeding someone's ego and making someone very, very rich. Many leaders living in complete luxury and over the top extravagance from monies given by people to do God's work, it's disgusting and achieved by out and out deception. 1 Kings 18:21,(NIV) Elijah came near all the people and said "how long will you go limping with two different opinions? If the Lord is God follow Him; but if it is Baal, then follow him." I believe that God is saying to the church today "Do you chose me or Baal, make up your mind, you can't have both". When King Herod killed off all the boys of two years and under in the area where Jesus was born as he wanted to make sure he got the Lord, but he missed. Just like King Ahab, these men wanted the glory for themselves and they weren't going to let anybody take that from them, not even God himself! Oh boy, were they so wrong.

How utterly pathetic can you get? How utterly deceived can you get? It reminds me of many of the false apostles in the church today with their luxurious life styles that reek of the world and the system of the world. Drawing away so many of God's people, which I believe is such a sad situation, which have itching ears to hear the garbage that comes out of their mouths. They come as an angel of light and so does Satan! When Jesus went into the temple, it was the place that gentiles could go into as well and seeing what was going on, he was angry, very, very angry that the house of God had become nothing more than a place of enterprise, just like the world! Not only did the religious establishment rob God of true worship but also robbed the gentiles of a place where they could come and feel God's presence, thus leading some of them to make a commitment to him Mark 11:15-17 (NIV). Like so many of the churches today, with all of their riches and grandeur which turns so many people OFF! Let us build up resolve against this type of thing, 2 Corinthians 11:13-14. Oh let us get back the true anointing that has been usurped from us by lying spirits that say "This is the way walk ye in it." Jesus said he would build the church and nothing, I repeat nothing, will stop him and we must be open to the way He wants it built!

# 22

# Good Seed and Bad Seed

When I first came to the Lord, just after Easter 1969, the Lord was bringing in a wave of worship that many older Christians had not been involved in before. Much of the teaching was how to do this and with it was a cost. There was a real hunger and thirst for God to manifest Himself in the church in a greater way, which was great! But with this, false apostles rose up with this move, now Jesus did say this would happen! Matthew 13:24-30 (NIV) it's about a parable of good seed and bad seed; how a man sowed good seed but the enemy came along and sowed bad seed as well. Verse 25 says when everyone was sleeping the bad seed was sown. Boy oh boy this is something to be so careful about; we must be on guard against this type of thing, putting on the whole armour of God. False apostles, prophets, teachers, etc come as angels of light and much of their doctrine sounds so good but all its doing is appealing to the flesh. We the church must get to a place of knowing which is false and which is truth. We must allow God to wake us up and to sharpen our spiritual senses, getting to a place that nothing else satisfies, only that which is of Him! We must do this by repentance for being slack, by the way we have tried to bring in His presence, not only for ourselves but also the church and nation, we need to get on our knees and seek God in prayer and fasting and get into HIS word, the true anointed word of God, rightly dividing it so as to take us on in liberty and truth.

# 23

# Bringing Again the Acceptable Sacrifice

David only used the right stones out of the brook to overcome Goliath, the ones that were prepared by the water, the true word of God. God will only accept the true anointed word as He did when Elijah poured out the acceptable water, (the word, and we must remember water, God's word, was very scarce because there was a drought in the land but not to the anointed of God.) over the sacrifice that was offered to our Lord. The bible goes on to say the fire of God licked up the water in the trench that was dug round about the sacrifice! There was an abundance of it, and not only the water, God's anointed word, but the rocks as well; the ones that were used to build the altar, there were twelve of them, which is representative of the nation of Israel and the twelve tribes. God used this to show that He will bring a unity, a true unity to the church by His spirit and truth in the last days. At the time of that sacrifice Israel was divided into two kingdoms, north and south. The fire also consumed the wood that was used to burn the sacrifice or the cross of Christ which is the only way for all of us to come into a true understanding of what the kingdom of God is all about. God will only reveal His plans to humble hearts, by the way of the cross. The bullock, which was to be sacrificed, represents the Baals of this world, false religions. As God the Father reveals to us our hearts and the gods that we hang on to, we must put them on the altar so the Lord can deal with them to take us on with him into greater glory. The bible goes on to say that the dust round about the sacrifice, which speaks of the flesh of man, was also burnt up. Because we have been made from the dust of the earth, and because of sin which has so corrupted us, no flesh will ever glory before God. The fire that God sent down from heaven consumed all of Elijah's sacrifice showing us that God will only accept true worship, in spirit and in truth and not the way of Baal, 1 Kings 18:38. All this was written as a type for us latter day saints to see and take note of!

John 12:1-8 tells us Jesus went to Lazarus' place where they made Him a supper and Martha served! Mary on the other hand anointed the feet of Jesus with very costly ointment of pure spikenard and wiped His feet with her hair. For a Jewish woman to do that showed that she understood who Jesus was and she humbled herself and brought a true sacrifice, one with humility and one that cost a lot. The bible goes on to say that the house was filled with the fragrance of that sacrifice! Mary had learned to sit at Jesus' feet and hear what the Spirit was saying through Him. Martha again was caught up in doing, doing, doing and not taking time out to hear what the Lord was saying. This is what we the church must get back to, hearing what God is saying. There has been so much junk and rubbish fed to the church that we must wake up to what's going on and allow God to deal with it; we must allow God to get rid of the dirty muddied water (the wrong word, the way of the world) by which so much of the church has tried to use to bring in God's glory with! We must get back to the clean, pure, fantastic, great and mighty waters that bring in true repentance and a true born again relationship with our Saviour and Lord. The LIVING WATER of the anointed word, to bring in again the fragrance that will fill God's house and is acceptable to Him! We must get back in determination and desperation of wanting God's glory back in the church as Hannah, in 1 Samuel 1:18 showed when she cried out in her heart to the Lord for a son. She was outside the tent of the meeting, where the Ark of the Covenant was kept. The high priest of the day thought she was drunk because she was so distressed and seemed to be acting like a loony and her lips were not moving, but in her heart she was crying out to the Lord. God revealed to Eli the high priest that he was going to give her what she had prayed for. Like the woman with an issue of blood that wanted Jesus to heal her, she pushed through the onlookers to get what she needed and Jesus sensed it and her faith healed her, Luke 8:43-48 or the Canaanite woman in Matthew 15:21-28 who wanted Jesus to cast out an evil spirit from her daughter! Jesus tested her faith, but she persisted and got what she asked for. All these ladies were determined, and rightly so, to get God to do something that was needed in their lives and God used it for His glory. We need to start to reclaim what has been lost in the church, allowing God to reveal truth back to us but there is a cost to this and we must be willing to pay it if we want to share in His glory.

Matthew 13:37-41 (NIV) "As the weeds are pulled up and burned in the fire, so it will be at the end of the age. The Son of Man will send out his angels and they will weed out of His kingdom everything that causes sin and all who are evil". Angels speaks of messengers, I believe God is rising up people that know their God, and will bring a message or word that will drown out the false junk that has been feed to us by false ministries! I believe He is bringing back a hunger and thirst to His people that only he can fill! He is calling His sons and daughters out of the pig pens that have so captivated many of them and saying repent, come back to the first love that we have so easily let slip. I believe we have all been there in one degree or another, and He is saying to all of us, "Come back My beloved, come My love; come back to My garden and taste again of My precious fruit, the only fruit that can satisfy your soul. The fig tree has put forth its figs and the vines are in blossom which gives forth fragrance, arise My love, my fair one and come away with Me. Oh My love, My bride I want to bring you into My banqueting house and My banner over you is love. Do not allow the foxes, the little foxes, spoil again the vineyards, for once more the vineyard is in blossom. Again I will put on your finger My ring, on your person My best robe and on your feet sandals to let you know I see you as My bride, my beautiful one that I shed My blood for, for you were dead and now alive, was lost but now found and once more walk with you in the cool of the day, not only as My friend but as My bride".

Let us wake up oh bride of Christ and have ears to hear what the Holy Spirit is saying to the churches, the bridegroom is coming for those that are ready to receive Him! ARE YOU??

www.ingramcontent.com/pod-product-compliance
Lightning Source LLC
Chambersburg PA
CBHW051946290426
44110CB00015B/2134